Building
LEADERSHIP
Talent

ENDORSEMENTS

Leadership is not a static concept, especially in a disruptive and connected world. It is complex and multi-dimensional. It needs to be understood and applied at contextual, operational and micro levels. Certainly it is much more than a set of competencies.

More has probably been written and spoken about leadership than almost any other topic throughout history. However, to understand leadership is to understand the concept from multiple perspectives. That is what this very comprehensive book provides. There is no single approach to leadership and the variety of perspectives provided in this book will further enhance our understanding and practice of leadership.

An important book with highly qualified and insightful contributors which will add to the conversations about leadership for a long time to come. An essential read for leaders and those responsible for leadership in their organisations now and in the future.

Terry Meyer, Strategy & Leadership Consultant, Leadership SA

Truly a standout book that packs a real punch in the sea of books on leadership. This extraordinary book has to be the most updated, and most comprehensive and definitive compendium on leaders and leadership, written by an impressive array of prominent and respected experts in the field.

Understanding the "what" and "how" of leadership is something that most organisations continue to grapple with in these volatile, complex, uncertain and ambiguous times. This book offers advice on the toughest challenges leaders are facing in business today.

This is compulsory reading for anyone seeking to understand and distil powerful perspectives on leadership and how to become a better leader.

The book provides robust perspectives on leadership fundamentals ranging from leadership theory, models and frameworks on leadership, leadership principles and philosophy, and, in addition, offers authentic, actionable examples. It is bursting with great tips and advice that are immediately applicable and anchored in research.

An indispensable and essential resource for leaders and aspiring leaders at all levels.

Shirley Zinn, Professor Shirley Zinn, Group HR Director, Woolworths

This book is rooted in the challenges facing leaders today, and offers current and future leaders a perspective to help them lead in a VUCA world. The authors take a unique view of leadership from a "value chain" perspective. They provide executives and those in the leadership development business a framework and insight into both being and building better leaders for tomorrow. I believe this book – a product of frontline leaders – will prove to be a great handbook for those who regard leadership as both an interest and a passion.

Paul Norman, MTN Group: Group Human Resources and Corporate Affairs Officer

I have read dozens of books on leadership but none of them has tackled this complex topic in the way that *Building Leadership Talent* has done. This book tackles the real issues of leadership from understanding the foundations of leadership; to examining leadership within its unfolding context; to leadership identification, growth and development to issues of leadership transitions and leadership wellbeing. The insights and models are based on research and on real experiences and I particularly enjoyed the section on leadership articles and stories – real-life leadership experiences as told by the leaders themselves.

This book is that rare mix of a treasure house of up-to-date knowledge about every aspect of leadership and at the same time full of insights and suggestions for practical implementation. It is both thought-provoking and enlightening, and a must-read for anyone trying to understand the complex issues surrounding leadership. This is one of the best books on the topic of leadership I have been privileged to read.

Italia Boninelli, HR Strategist, Executive Coach and Author, (recent past Executive Vice-president: People and Organizational Development, AngloGold Ashanti)

The seminal guide to the kind of transformational leadership required in the 21st century and beyond.

S'ne Mkhize, Senior Vice President, Human Resources – Sasol

What a phenomenal work!

This is the most comprehensive, insightful and well-grounded work on leadership ever published in South Africa.

It unpacks leadership in its many facets and perspectives – from individual to organisational and global leadership.

The authors are thought leaders, scientists and subject-matter experts; they ask the difficult questions and reveal the essence of leadership as an art and science.

This book is a must for everybody in leadership positions – be it the business sector, public sector, religious organisations, education, or community organisations.

An ideal reference work for the consultant or business science practitioner.

Dr Johan de Beer, Human Capital Executive, Africa Division, Imperial Logistics

Building Leadership Talent is a feast for scholars, students and practitioners alike who will find a comprehensive reference book on leadership theories, a diversity of the schools of thought that have influenced and continue to shape the evolution of leadership as a fully fledged discipline that is applied to complex and changing contexts. As someone trying to master the leadership discipline and as an aspirant leadership expert myself, I was pleasantly surprised at how much there is still to know and learn about this enthralling subject called leadership.

Dudu Msomi, Chief Executive Officer, Busara Leadership Partners

Given the plethora of books on Leadership, one is tempted to think, "What else can be written about leadership?"

This masterful creation crushes that thought. It is a call to choose to be a different and better leader, to stand up and … lead.

I recommend that current and future leaders, young and old, study this gem and weave the learnings into their approach to leading our most precious asset, people.

Leon Steyn, Group Human Resources Executive, Bidvest

First published in 2017

ISBN: 978-1-86922-692-3 (Printed)
ISBN:978-1-86922-693-0 (ePDF)

Published by KR Publishing
P O Box 3954
Randburg
2125
Republic of South Africa

Tel: (011) 706-6009
Fax: (011) 706-1127
E-mail: orders@knowres.co.za
Website: www.kr.co.za

Printed and bound: HartWood Digital Printing, 243 Alexandra Avenue, Halfway House, Midrand
Typesetting, layout and design: Cia Joubert, cia@knowres.co.za
Cover design: Marlene de'Lorme, marlene@knowres.co.za and Cia Joubert, cia@knowres.co.za
Editing: Adrienne Pretorius, pretorii@mweb.co.za
Proofreading: Valda Strauss: valda@global.co.za
Project management: Cia Joubert, cia@knowres.co.za

Building

LEADERSHIP

Talent

Edited by

Theo H Veldsman and Andrew J Johnson

kr
publishing

2017

ACKNOWLEDGEMENTS

What a pleasure to work with authors who see the unquestionable criticality of leadership, and are passionate about the difference leadership must make in assuring a desirable, sustainable future for all. It was wonderful to have worked with each and every one of our 69 authors over such an extended period of time. Your wisdom, expertise, suggestions and time willingly shared in crafting your invaluable contribution in making *Building Leadership Talent* the outstanding and trend-setting Thought Leadership Book it has turned out to be is gratefully acknowledged.

A warm word of thanks is due to:

- All of our Peer Reviewers for your valuable input and time.
- To all our Endorsees for your time given, to offer our book the cachet it deserves.
- Wilhelm Crous, Managing Director of KR, for your constant stretch and guidance; constructive criticism; ongoing encouragement; infectious enthusiasm; and advice and help in working around and through barriers, that made it such a pleasure to work on our book.
- Joann Hill for organising the peer reviews and endorsements.
- Cia Joubert, for your excellent project management of our book that was mission critical in ensuring that the right things happened at the right time and in the right way so that our book became a reality.
- Adrienne Pretorius, our technical editor, for ensuring the technical quality excellence of our book.
- Valda Strauss, for the excellent proofreading of our book after layout.

Last but not least, a warm, appreciative "Thank you" to our families for their understanding, support and sacrifices throughout the painful birth process of the book which took two years from initiation, through conceptualisation and production, to final delivery.

TABLE OF CONTENTS

FOREWORD BY PROF SHIRLEY ZINN

We all know that leadership is critical to the success of the world, society, businesses and organisations. Millions of books, blogs, articles have been written over hundreds of years on the topic of leadership, yet it remains a complex and vexing focus of debate to this day.

Building Leadership Talent comes at a time where we are grappling with how we strategically plan, identify and build our leadership pipelines and what the best strategies are to nurture leadership talent. How can our leadership change the world and build a better life for customers, clients, staff, and communities through thoughtful strategies that genuinely care about people, planet and profit?

I am truly humbled and honoured to be able to write this foreword on *Building Leadership Talent.* I write this foreword enthusiastically and with great excitement as we contemplate what leadership means in the 21st century and beyond.

Building Leadership Talent is an extraordinary effort to understand the complexities and challenges of how we should be strategically planning, identifying and building leadership talent as we enter the Fourth Industrial Revolution, and what inspirational and transformational leadership means in this context.

Building Leadership Talent is a must read for those aspiring to be dynamic and insightful leaders who are future-fit. It provides accessible tools and tips for sustainable success as a dynamic leader in a new era. It is a guide to what it means to be a responsive leader and provides stories, case studies, lesson learned and analytics for how as impactful leaders we might continue to improve ourselves and grow a fresh cadre of leaders who can meaningfully build a better world.

Building Leadership Talent is empowering, practical and grounded in research with easy to understand models, conceptual frameworks and practical, implementable advice. It is an engaging read that will enable measurable results. It will challenge you to develop the leader in yourself and others. It is visionary, values-driven and premised on success through purpose.

This read will challenge all conventional wisdom of leadership and provide a fresh perspective of what the future will require from leaders. Transformational leadership and the ability to grow leadership with the attributes to rise above the old command and control mindset to what it means to make a difference to humanity, and to live in service to others. This book challenges leaders to make every action and every decision count.

We are called upon to develop our youth to evolve into the leaders of the future who lead with impact. In doing so we have to reflect on ethical and responsible leadership and how we develop young leaders so that we strengthen our leadership pipeline. We also have to consider what it means to be a leader currently and into the future, and how to do this with authenticy, determination, passion and diligence.

Building Leadership Talent enables us to learn from the wisdom of those who came before us, how they "did it", sacrifices made, transition points and how they rose to the challenges of the day. It affords us the opportunity to engage with leadership principles that have risen to the test of time and to learn from them. It cuts through the clutter and the noise, and helps to catapult our thinking on growing deep and wide leadership talent and how to produce results through people.

This is a unique and compelling read as our organisations and businesses become increasingly complex and our world is calling out for leaders who care, take responsibility for positive change and who truly want to make a difference.

Prof Shirley Zinn, Group Head of Human Resources, Woolworths Holdings Ltd; and bestselling author of 'Swimming Upstream'

ABOUT THE EDITORS

Prof Theo H Veldsman

Theo, who is regarded as a thought leader in South Africa with respect to people management and the psychology of work, has demonstrated his ability to proactively identify emerging people and leadership needs and arrive at fit-for-purpose, innovative solutions that are theoretically and practically sound.

Theo holds a PhD in Industrial Psychology and is a registered Industrial Psychologist and Research Psychologist and accredited HRM Practitioner. He prefers to call himself a Work Psychologist. He has extensive research and development, as well as consulting experience gained over the past 35 years in strategy formulation and implementation; strategic organisational change; organisational (re)design; team building; leadership/management and strategic people/talent management. He consults with many leading South African companies as well as organisations overseas, in the roles of advisor, expert and coach/mentor.

In addition to being the author of nearly 200 technical/consulting reports/articles, he has done numerous management and professional presentations and attended seminars at a national and international level. He is the author of two books, and has contributed nine book chapters.

Up to the end of 2016, when he retired, he was Professor and Head of the Department of Industrial Psychology and People Management, Faculty of Management, University of Johannesburg. Since the beginning of 2017 he is a Visiting Professor at the sam eDepartment. He has led the profession of Psychology and Industrial Psychology nationally as president on several occasions. He has been awarded fellowship status by the Society of Industrial and Organisational Psychology of South Africa (SIOPSA), and is the 2012 recipient of a Life-Long Achievement Award from the South African Board for People Practices (SABPP).

Dr Andrew J Johnson

Andrew is the Chief Learning Officer at Eskom's Academy of Learning. An Industrial Psychologist by profession, he holds an MSc in Occupational Psychology (Nottingham) and a PhD in Industrial Psychology from the University of Johannesburg (UJ). He has also completed formal philosophical, theological and exegetical studies at Sts. Peter & John Vianney Seminaries and St Joseph's Scholasticate.

A seasoned HR executive, his special interests are HR strategy consulting, leadership development, talent and succession management, organisational transformation, and change management. His career in Organisational Effectiveness in the private sector has seen him working for Edcon, MTN, Avmin, JSE and Liberty in senior positions, and he has consulted to other state-owned entities, private companies, and African and BRICS (Brazil, Russia, India, China and South Africa) utilities.

He held non-executive roles in FASSET, the NEF, the COJ Property Company, Transparency SA, NSFAS, & King II; currently he serves on the Advisory Committee of the Industrial Psychology Department of UJ (where he is an occasional lecturer), and the HR (Staffing) Committee of the University of KwaZulu-Natal (UKZN). Andrew is involved in the Society for Industrial & Organisational Psychology of South Africa (SIOPSA) (president in 2011/12), and the Global Forum on Executive Development and Business Driven Action Learning. He is the winner of the prestigious IPM HR Director of the Year (2014), and the recipient of the SABPP Lifetime Achievement Award (2014) and of SIOPSA's Honorary Life Membership (2012).

He is in high demand as a speaker, coach and mentor. At his core he is a deeply passionate student of human behaviour in the context of work, and how this can create a better self, team, organisation and society.

ABOUT THE CONTRIBUTORS

Jens Baier

Jens is a partner and Managing Director in BCG's Düsseldorf office. He is a core member of BCG's People and Organisation practice. E-mail: baier.jens@bcg.com

Sharmla Chetty

Sharmla is the Global Head of Europe and Africa for Duke Corporate Education and serves on the board for Duke Corporate Education (CE) Africa. She leads the client relationship management potfolio, advisory work, and the building of client organisations' strategic capacity and capabilities. She has experience working in financial services, healthcare and mining in Africa, China, Europe and India. Prior to joining Duke CE, Sharmla was head of Human Capital Development at Nedbank and has more than 19 years' experience in this field.

Sharmla studied at Rand Afrikaans University (RAU) and has an MBA from Henley Management Business School. Not only did her dissertation in the field of corporate social responsibility receive a distinction, she was also the recipient of the 2016 Award for Entrepreneurial and Academic Excellence on the African continent. A Fellow of the eighth class of the Africa Leadership Initiative-South Africa, she is a member of the Aspen Global Leadership Network.

David Conradie

David commenced his career in the financial services industry in 1990, working as an intern Industrial Psychologist and thereafter in HR management-related roles, ranging from group psychologist to HR executive.

Having joined Deloitte Consulting in 2000, he most recently held the position of partner in the Human Capital Service Line. He served as Project Director of the annual Deloitte Best Company to Work For survey, and as leader of both the Talent Management and Leadership Centres of Excellence. From 2008–2012 David was a member of the Deloitte Consulting Global Talent Steering Committee, overseeing the conceptualisation, development and global roll-out of the firm's Talent Management consulting methodologies and related thought leadership publications. In 2012 he was appointed Global Human Capital Leader for Talent Analytics, where he led the successful launch and expansion of the firm's human capital market offerings into Africa.

In 2013 David joined Top Talent Solutions (Pty) Ltd, a specialist I/O Psychology Consulting firm, as Executive Head of its Leadership Academy. He also served as Principal: Talent and Leadership where he was active in the design, development, delivery and project management of a range of advisory services to clients across Africa, the Indian Ocean Islands and South East Asia.

David is currently Key Account Director for Mindcor Consulting. His areas of specialisation include strategic talent management, leadership succession planning and management, leadership assessment and development, employee engagement and employer branding.

David holds a Master of Arts (cum laude) in Industrial Psychology from the University of the Witwatersrand (Wits). He is a registered Industrial Psychologist with the South African Health Professions Council, a full member of the Society for Industrial and Organisational Psychology of South Africa, and is Chairman of the Membership and Professional Designation Committee of the Institute of People Management.

Christel Fourie

Christel holds a DPhil (Industrial Psychology) from the University of Johannesburg. This chapter is based on her thesis, *The FirstRand founders' story: Exploring synergistic relationships*. The founders are prominent business leaders, and her research pivoted on how effective leaders shape organisational culture.

As an Industrial Psychologist, Christel focuses on identifying and developing talent. She has held senior consulting positions at SHL (now CEB) and JvR Consulting Psychologists. Her clients, who represent different sectors, include Nedcor, Telkom, Swiss Re, HP and FNB. Christel lived in Japan from 2008 to 2013, where she volunteered as a phone counsellor at the Tokyo English Lifeline. This experience honed her counselling skills and deepened her understanding of wellbeing, change, cultural adjustment and expatriates.

Christel currently lives in London with her family. She often recalls a leadership pipeline cornerstone: *Lead and manage the self before managing others*. It seems equally applicable to parenting.

Adriaan Groenewald

Adriaan is South Africa's foremost leadership commentator and Managing Director of Leadership Platform. He holds a Bachelor's in Psychology and Criminology and a postgraduate business qualification. His career spans from management in large corporates to establishing Leadership Platform, where he advises and consults with top leaders.

Not only has Adriaan authored and co-authored three books on leadership, over more than 15 years he has also interviewed hundreds of leaders from across the spectrum – including President Jacob Zuma, Adrian Gore, Steven R Covey, Gary Player and Thuli Madonsela – to understand why they succeeded or failed in certain respects. He produces and hosts radio shows – currently a weekly three-hour, Leadership Transformation Platform show on CliffCentral.com, where he continues to interview top leaders.

Adriaan believes in being fit: physically, spiritually, emotionally, mentally – and especially leadership fit. A family man with a Second Dan black belt in karate, he loves the bush and serving the community.

Nancy Keeshan

As Executive Director in Duke CE's Learning Solutions Design Group, Nancy works with clients on all aspects of talent development, including the creation of a talent pipeline architecture outlining programmatic and non-programmatic development options at multiple levels within an organisation. She also designs and delivers customised educational initiatives, specialising in immersive and experiential learning activities.

Philipp Kolo

A principal in the Munich office of the Boston Consulting Group, Philipp is a topic expert in learning and development and a core member of the firm's People and Organisation practice. E-mail: kolo.philipp@bcg.com

Piet Naudé

Piet holds an MA in Philosophy and a DTh in Theology. He is Professor of Ethics and former Deputy Vice-Chancellor: Academic of Nelson Mandela Metropolitan University in Port Elizabeth, South Africa. He was appointed as Director of the University of Stellenbosch Business School (USB) in September 2014. Piet is a National Research Foundation rated scholar who has published widely in both academic journals and the popular media.

Aletta Odendaal

Aletta completed a BA in Social Work (Potchefstroom University for Christian Higher Education), a BA (Hons) in Industrial Psychology (University of South Africa), an MPhil (cum laude) in Industrial Psychology (Rand Afrikaans University) and a DPhil in Industrial Psychology (University of Johannesburg [UJ]). A registered Industrial Psychologist, she is a Master HR Professional. The current Qualification Leader for the MPhil in Leadership Coaching at UJ, she has more than 18 years' experience in strategic executive leadership development, executive coaching and psychological assessment interventions across all levels in different organisations, including mining, retail, engineering, academic institutions, government, NGOs, media and communications.

Her research interests include psychological assessment, leadership development and coaching psychology. She has presented papers at national and international conferences, published research results in academic journals and co-edited two books. Her passion for, and commitment to, Industrial Psychology, leading testing practices and the development of coaching psychology are evident: she served as President of the Society for Industrial and Organisational Psychology of South Africa (2002–2006), Chair of People Assessment in Industry (2008–2011) and was awarded Honorary Membership (2006), received a Presidential Award for the development of coaching psychology (2012) and a fellowship (2015). She was elected to the Council of the International Test Commission (2010) and currently serves as Secretary-General. Aletta is a founder member of the Interest Group in Coaching and Consulting Psychology and she participated in the Global Convention of Coaching in New York (2007) and Dublin (2008). She is a member of the International Steering Committee and Honorary Vice-President of the International Society of Coaching Psychology. See Aletta@odendaalconsulting.co.za

Rainer Strack

Rainer is Senior Partner and Managing Director in BCG's Düsseldorf office. He is the leader of the People and Organisation practice in Europe and the worldwide topic leader for the firm's work in human resources. E-mail: strack.rainer@bcg.com

Nicola Taylor

Nicola Taylor obtained her undergraduate BSc and Honours in Psychology at the University of Stellenbosch before moving to Johannesburg to complete her MSc and PhD (Psychology) at the University of Johannesburg. She also completed her internship as a psychometrist at the Institute for Child and Adult Guidance. In 2005, she took part in a research exchange programme with the Rijksuniversiteit Groningen, in the Netherlands.

Nicola is Director at JvR Psychometrics (JvR), where she heads up the Research Department. She is responsible for managing the evaluation of the psychometric assessments distributed by JvR in terms of their appropriateness in the South African context. Nicola often conducts research with organisations in order to determine the effectiveness of programmes or the assessments used within an organisation. She has co-authored articles published in peer-reviewed journals, contributed to book chapters, and read a number of papers at local and international conferences. Her research focus is on cross-cultural psychological assessment, particularly within the field of personality assessment, test construction and the validation of psychometric assessments in the South African context. E-mail: nicola@jvrafrica.co.za

Paul Vorster

Paul earned a bachelor's degree in Psychology (cum laude) in 2008 and completed an honours in Industrial and Organisational (I/O) Psychology (cum laude) in 2009. He subsequently completed a Master of Philosophy in I/O Psychology (cum laude) at the University of Johannesburg (2010).

He specialises in psychometric assessment and psychological research, and works in areas of applied research, psychometrics, test-development, safety, employee selection and assessment. From 2011–2012 Paul worked at JvR Psychometrics where he focused on applied organisational research, test construction and psychometric assessment. He returned to academia from 2013–2014 to pursue a PhD in I/O Psychology with a focus on computer-adaptive testing of personality.

His primary areas of interest include quantitative research, factor analysis, computer-adaptive testing, item response theory, personality psychology and applied research. Paul returned to JvR Psychometrics in 2015 as an I/O Psychologist while completing his PhD part-time, specialising in psychometric research and facilitating training on ethics, Myers-Briggs Type Indicator (MBTI) accreditation training and Hogan Assessment Suite accreditation training. He also consults in areas of organisational development. Paul has presented scientific papers at the International Conference of Psychology, the International Congress of Cross-Cultural Psychology, and the Annual Conference of the International Test Commission. He is a founding member of the World Congress of Personality, which specialises in the scientific study and progression of personality theory and its applications throughout the world. He has recently obtained his PhD from the University of Johannesburg in Industrial and Organisatinal (I/O) Psychology.

SECTION 1
SETTING THE SCENE

Chapter 1

ORIENTATION

Theo H Veldsman and Andrew J Johnson

On many fronts, and in many ways, our insight into and the exercise of leadership is under severe scrutiny because of a radically changing and significantly different world; reinventing organisations; and working persons with significantly different, or significantly shifting, needs, expectations and aspirations. Without doubt, leadership is in the overheating crucible of a reframed/reframing world that is in the throes of fundamental and radical transformation.

The current fierce debate about leadership and leadership excellence (or lack thereof) may be one of the most important issues of our present time, alongside issues such as demographic shifts, the distribution of economic prosperity, food and water security, world peace, global warming, and sustainability. It could even be argued that these issues in and of themselves are but symptomatic of poor leadership; or, at worst, of the inability and/or a lack in the commitment to lead.

The clarion call is clear and unequivocal. At this critical juncture in our history, the search is on for better *and* different leadership. Leaders and leadership have to reinvent themselves if they wish to be successful in the unfolding world of tomorrow. Old recipes and conventional ways of leading will no longer suffice. They may even be detrimental and destructive. It can be argued that those nations, societies, communities and organisations that are able to demonstrate leadership excellence consistently will dominate and inherit the future, in particular in the case of emerging countries in Africa. Our very future is predicated on the quality of our current and future leadership who will either make us architects or victims of the future.

Without any doubt leadership is *the* critical strategic capability of nations, societies, communities and organisations, making them sustainably future-fit. The primary trigger for *Building Leadership Talent* is therefore to be found in the snowballing crisis around leadership, and the consequential imperative for better and different leadership.

The Strategic Leadership Value Chain Perspective: A Meta-framework From Which to View Leadership

Leadership is a critical organisational capability and intervention. To the best of our knowledge no overall, systemic, integrated and holistic perspective is available in the literature viewing leadership from a Strategic Leadership Value Chain perspective. Such a perspective would provide a meta-framework from which to look at leadership systemically and holistically as an organisational intervention. Such a perspective would assist one not only in bringing order to the overwhelming, exploding leadership literature, but also serve as an overall, integrative map for organisations in engaging with leadership. At best numerous, piecemeal treatises are available dealing with specialised leadership intervention topics, e.g. leadership assessment, leadership development, or leadership well-being but no overarching meta-framework exists.

Figure 1.1 provides our take on the make-up of the Strategic Leadership Value Chain in terms of which leadership as a mission-critical, strategic organisational capability and intervention can be viewed.

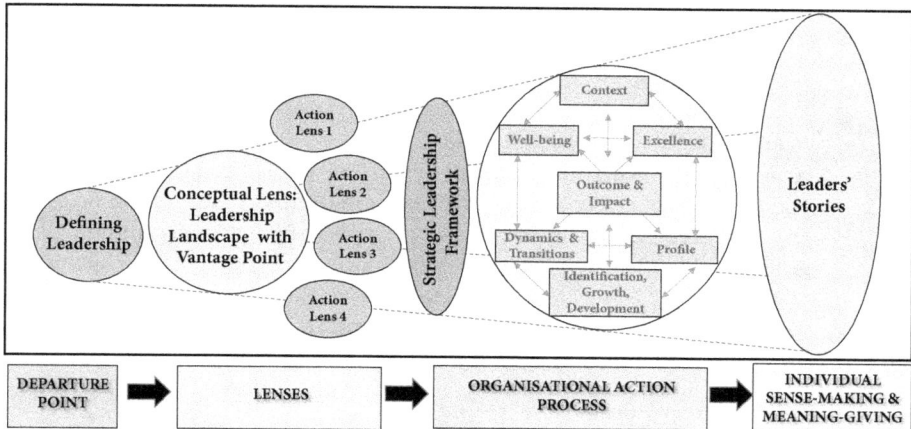

Figure 1.1 A Strategic Leadership Value Chain Perspective on leadership as an organisational capability and intervention

The make-up of the Strategic Leadership Value Chain

With reference to Figure 1.1, the Strategic Leadership Value Chain is composed of the following elements:

- **Departure point: Defining leadership**

  In crafting an organisation-specific leadership thinking framework, the organisation as a starting point must formulate explicitly and intentionally what they understand "leadership" as a phenomenon to be conceptually, in order to correctly demarcate the territory called "leadership". An incorrect definition of leadership can delineate the phenomenon either too narrowly, consequently excluding essential elements of leadership; or too broadly, resulting in the inclusion of unrelated elements ("noise") in its definition.

- **Lenses**

  Having demarcated the territory called "leadership" by defining it, the organisation must next construct and/or select the lenses it will use to map, make sense of, and give meaning to the demarcated leadership territory. The lenses represent the "toolbox" the organisation will use in engaging with the leadership territory. Three types of lenses can be discerned:

  o **Conceptual lens:** This represents the organisation's meta-view – its "Google map" - of what building blocks (= "towns with their suburbs") with their interdependencies (= "roads") make up the demarcated leadership territory. We call this meta-conceptual view the *"Leadership Landscape"*.

    The value of the Leadership Landscape as meta-conceptual view of the leadership territory is three-fold:

    - *to simplify*, organise and integrate at a meta-level the complexity of the field of leadership with its ever-expanding and overwhelming literature;

    - *to provide* a common meta-language for an all-inclusive, coherent leadership dialogue about leadership, for example in teaching, or in an organisation; and

    - *to structure* an organisation's conversation about leadership, enabling it to arrive at a customised Strategic Leadership Framework (see below) for the organisation that will direct and guide its thinking, decisions and actions regarding leadership as a strategic organisational capability and intervention.

o *Interpretative Lens:* A Vantage Point next must be chosen by which the Leadership Landscape with its building blocks will be interpreted. For example, Appreciative Inquiry or Critical Management Theory.

o *Action Lenses:* Having mapped the leadership territory, and having chosen a Vantage Point, the Action Lenses serve as enabling tools selected by the organisation to deal and work with the various building blocks making up the Leadership Landscape. Action tools represent various disciplines and theoretical/practical approaches that can be used to engage with the leadership territory in order to make sense of it. Examples of such action tools are neuroscience, action science, psychodynamics, narratives, and psychobiographical profiling.

- *Strategic leadership framework*

In proceeding along the Strategic Leadership Value Chain (see Figure 1.1), the organisation next has to make choices regarding its specific position on each of the building blocks making up the Leadership Landscape as Conceptual Lens, based on how it strategically wants to position leadership in its organisation.

For example with respect to some of the building blocks of the Leadership Landscape (given in italics), the choices are:

o Its chosen *Leadership Stance* regarding leadership for the organisation: Does leadership need to be task- and/or people-centric? Must leadership be present and/or future focused?

o Its desired *Leadership Style(s)*: Tell, Consultative, Co-determination and/or Self-Governance?

o Its repertoire of expected *Leadership Roles*: Resources, Coach, Guide, Networker?

o Leadership Talent Management: its make-up; strategic talent timeframe; and talent pools.

The Strategic Leadership Framework therefore forms the reference point and basis regarding all the organisation's decisions and actions with respect to leadership. Its sits as a bridge between the organisation's Leadership Thinking Framework on the one hand, being part of the Thinking Framework itself. And, on the other hand, the Framework directs and guides how "things" must happen in the organisation with respect to leadership.

- *Organisational action processes*

The organisational action process refers to the frontline decisions and actions the organisation has to take on a daily basis regarding leadership. This process is made up of an integrated, reciprocally interdependent, set of organisational actions, embedded in an organisational change navigation process (represented in Figure 1.1 by the circle in which these actions are contained). The actions are as follows:

o *Action 1:* Understanding the unfolding *Leadership Context* with its leadership challenges, demands and requirements;

o *Action 2:* Formulating a context-relevant *Leadership Excellence* model;

o *Action 3:* Generating a future-fit *Leadership Brand and Profile*;

o *Action 4: Identifying, Growing and Developing* the organisation's leadership talent;

- o **Action 5:** Managing the ongoing, everyday *Leadership Dynamics and Transitions* in the organisation;
- o **Action 6:** Ensuring and enhancing *Leadership Wellbeing* (and countering leadership mal-being); and
- o **Action 7:** Monitoring and tracking *Leadership Outcomes and Impact*

- **Individual sense-making and meaning-giving: Leadership stories**

  In the final instance, leaders have to be prolific, enticing storytellers. Through the stories they construct and share, leaders make sense of and give meaning to their leadership experiences, for themselves and others. Hopefully and ideally speaking, leadership experiences are transformed into information; information into knowledge; and knowledge into wisdom. In turn, the distilled wisdom can be applied to ground, enhance and enrich in a recursive fashion the preceding Strategic Leadership Value Chain elements as elucidated above.

This book – *Building Leadership Talent* – forms part of a five book series covering the respective elements of the Strategic Leadership Value Chain. The accompanying box gives a list of the books in the series, and what portion of the Strategic Value Chain they address.

Book	Portion of Strategic Leadership Value Chain Addressed (Refer back to Figure 1.1)
Book 1: Understanding Leadership	Departure Point: Defining Leadership Lenses: Conceptual, Interpretive, Action Strategic Leadership Framework
Book 2: Leadership in Context	Organisational Action Process • *Action 1: Understanding the unfolding Leadership Context with its leadership challenges, demands and requirements*
Book 3: Leadership Excellence	Organisational Action Process • *Action 2: Formulating a context relevant, Leadership Excellence Model* • *Action 3: Generating a future-fit, Leadership Brand and Profile* • *Action 7: Monitoring and tracking Leadership Outcomes and Impact*
Book 4: Building Leadership Talent (This book)	Organisational Action Process • *Action 4: Identifying, growing and developing the organisation's leadership talent*
Book 5: Leadership Dynamics and Well Being	Organisational Action Process • *Action 5: Managing the ongoing, everyday Leadership Dynamics and Transitions in the organisation* • *Action 6: Ensuring and enhancing leadership well-being (and countering leadership mal-being)*

Book	Portion of Strategic Leadership Value Chain Addressed (Refer back to Figure 1.1)
Leadership Stories	Throughout the above five books stories by prominent SA leaders are given to illustrate how they have made sense of and given meaning to leadership

Purpose and Structure of *Building Leadership Talent*

The purpose of *Building Leadership Talent* is to address *Leadership Identification, Growth* and *Development* as action domain in the Organisational Action Process, premised on the desired Leadership Excellence, Brand and Profile as formulated within the other action domains. (To note: all of the actions making up the Organisational Action Process are encapsulated in an organisational change navigation process, represented in Figure 1.2 by the circle enclosing these actions).

The location of the Organisational Action Process within the Strategic Leadership Value Chain, and the action domain of Identification, Growth and Development, are indicated by arrows in Figure 1.2.

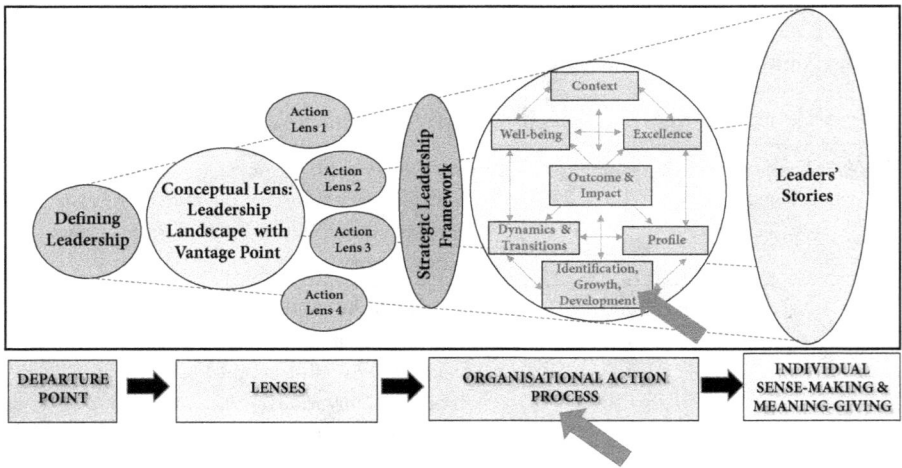

Figure 1.2 Organisational Action Process of the Strategic Leadership Value Chain: Identification, Growth and Development

Identification, Growth and Development form part of an integrated strategic leadership talent management process, necessary to build the organisation's strategic leadership pipeline. Such a talent management process is depicted in Figure 1.3.

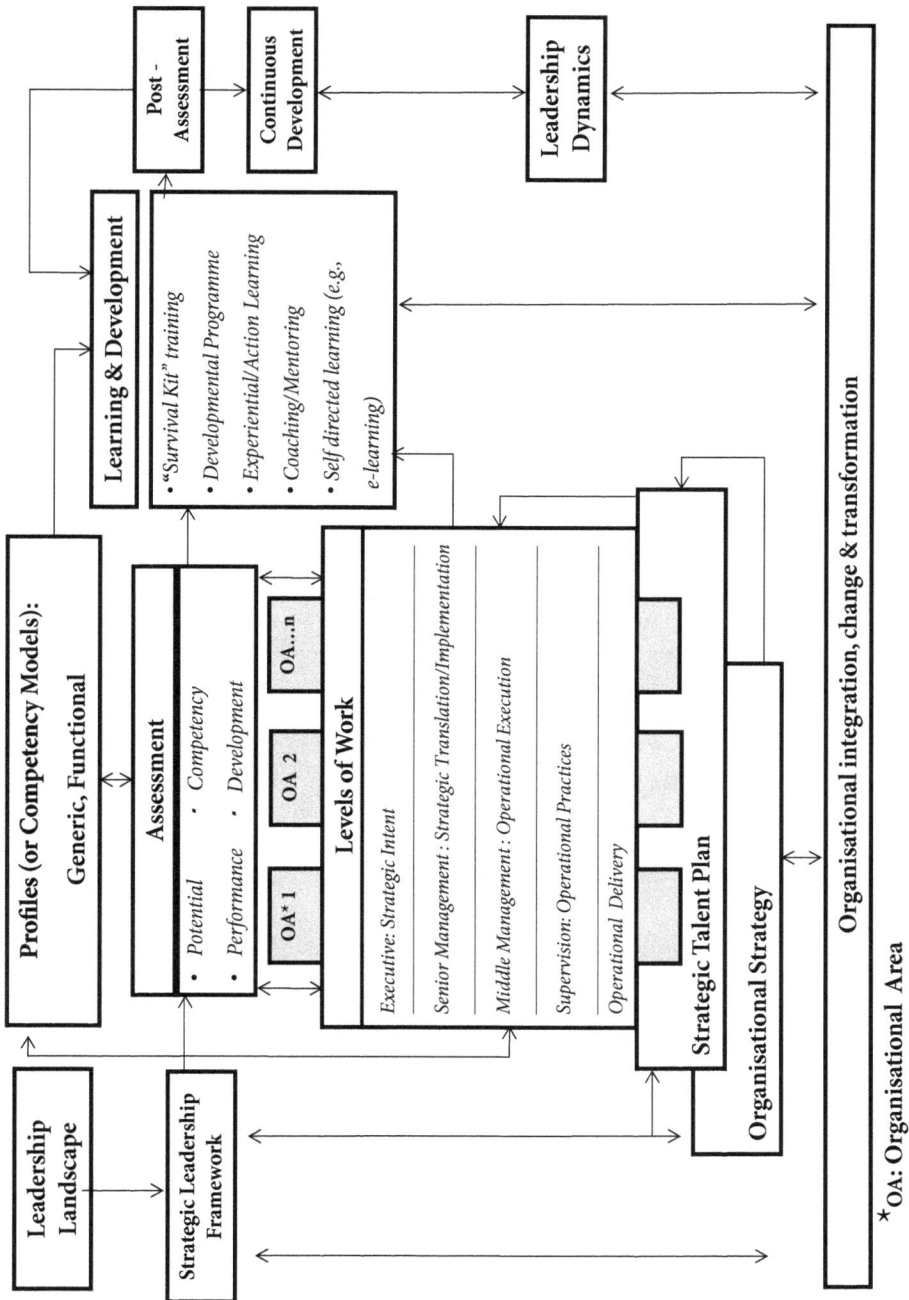

Figure 1.3 An integrated Strategic Leadership Talent Management Process

Based on the above discussion of the pertinent Action Process Step, and using Figure 1.3 as an organising framework, the topics addressed in *Building Leadership Talent* are given in the accompanying box.

SECTION	TOPICS ADDRESSED	LOCATION IN FIGURE 1.3	CHAPTER
Section 2: Requisite Leadership Capability	*Leadership talent for an uncertain future*	*Strategic Talent Plan*	*2*
Section 3: Leadership Assessment and Development	*Leadership assessment*	*Assessment*	*3*
	Leadership development: principles, approaches and processes	*Learning and Development*	*4*
	Leadership coaching	*Learning and Development*	*5*
Section 4: Leadership Types	*Business schools as hubs of leadership education*	*Learning and Development*	*6*
	Corporate universities	*Learning and Development*	*7*

Leadership Stories (Section 5: Chapter 8)

In this section prominent leaders express their personal views on leadership from the front line where it is happening for them, illustrating many of the topics discussed in *Building Leadership Talent*.

The future of leadership (Section 6: Chapter 9)

In this chapter we would like to gaze into the crystal ball by answering the question: Is there a need for better and different leadership going into the future? If yes, what would it look like with the conditions attached to such future-fit leadership?

Our intention with and aspirations for *Building Leadership Talent* – ambitious and bold, but humble

Our intention with and aspiration for *Building Leadership Talent* is for it to be a thought-leadership book on leadership at the front line in two ways. *Firstly*, by providing cutting edge, present-into-the-future, and future-into-the-present, thinking with respect to leadership lenses, leveraged from the best currently available insights and informed views about the expected probable future to be faced by leadership. *Secondly*, by providing actionable knowledge and theory-informed practice about leadership lenses where it matters at the organisational front line.

We realise we may be overly ambitious and bold both in our intention and aspiration by making the total Strategic Leadership Value Chain the focal point of *Building Leadership Talent*. Also, in covering in the comprehensive menu of topics what we believe are the most critical topics related to each element of the chain, while applying the Pareto principle of the 20% telling 80% of the story. Simultaneously, however, we are fortuitously humbled by the depth, richness and diversity of the overwhelming, exploding body of knowledge regarding leadership. In no way can we claim, or wish to claim, that at a topic level a high degree of seamless conceptual and practical integration within an element or across the total Strategic Leadership Value Chain exists. That would be arrogant.

The Intended Audience of *Building Leadership Talent*

In the first place, *Building Leadership Talent* intends to assist executives and leadership specialists within organisations, whether public or private, to direct, guide and build – confidently and with well-grounded insight – leadership as a mission critical organisational capability and intervention in their organisations, using a Strategic Leadership Value Chain perspective. In this way we hope that they will be able to ensure a future-fit organisation and leadership who are able and willing to be architects of the future they so ardently desire.

In the second place, *Building Leadership Talent* aims to assist academics and their students in the teaching and studying of leadership as a critically important subject. In the third place, the topics covered in *Building Leadership Talent* may also provide creative triggers to future leadership research.

The Intended Use of *Building Leadership Talent*

The intended use of *Building Leadership Talent* is to serve as a handy daily "desktop" reference book on leadership lenses to our intended audience:

- for ongoing referral as and when ways of understanding leadership matters arise in an organisation, and
- where input from a thought leadership source is desired and necessary on available leadership lenses.

Thus *Building Leadership Talent* is not intended to "Rest in Peace" on the bookshelf but to be a "Working Manual" by being an ever-present companion for continuous, daily consulting, referral and advice. Also in a similar fashion assist as a reference for teaching on and research into leadership.

The Expected Value-add of *Building Leadership Talent*

We hope *Building Leadership Talent* will provide you as the reader with six overriding insights (or Lessons-to-be-Learnt):

- Talent has become the *primary source of competitive advantage* in the unfolding Context. Assuring a sustainable supply of leaders at all levels therefore has become a key imperative for organisations globally.
- Leadership is a multifaceted construct that cannot be assessed using a single construct, or a single instrument. An *integrated, multi-component assessment approach* to leadership is required.

- In the emerging new order leadership needs to embrace different ways of perceiving the world; making sense of it; and catalysing action. *New angles to leadership development* have to be explored, conceived and implemented, like the three-stage leadership development process of perceiving, sense-making and choreography.
- *Leadership and executive coaching* has emerged globally as the most widely used intervention for leadership development.
- If Business Schools claim to be key centres of *"leadership education"*, they need to validate at least four critical areas of application: (1) self-leadership; (2) academic leadership; (3) executive leadership education; and (4) leading public discourse.
- Increasingly *Corporate Universities* – as set up within organisations – are being introduced as a major learning and development organisational vehicle to confront shrinking talent pools and to build strategically, critical skills timeously.

We wish you a stimulating, enriching and capacitating journey through *Building Leadership Talent*

SECTION 2

REQUISITE LEADERSHIP CAPABILITY

Chapter 2

LEADERSHIP TALENT FOR AN UNCERTAIN FUTURE

David Conradie

The successful attainment of an organisation's strategic intent ultimately depends on robust execution. This in turn is largely influenced by the organisation's ability to access a sustainable supply of the best possible leaders, both now and in the future. Confronted by continued economic pressure, increasingly competitive markets, and escalating stakeholder scrutiny of their leadership bench-strength, a growing number of organisations globally are realising that their future success will be severely compromised without the requisite leadership capability and capacity.

Despite widespread acknowledgement of the importance of leadership succession optimisation coupled with an increase in associated enabling investment, a significant number of business and HR executives believe that their organisations' efforts to produce a future supply of talented leaders are failing to deliver the desired outcomes. According to Deloitte, only 14% of the more than 7 000 respondents surveyed for the annual *Global Human Capital Trends Report 2016* believe that their organisations are "strong" at leadership succession planning, indicating a looming leadership capacity deficit.[1]

Similarly, only 15% of organisations participating in the Development Dimensions International Global Leadership Forecast 2014/2015 rated their future leadership bench-strength as strong, representing a decrease of 3% from the 2012/2013 Forecast.[2] A study conducted by KPMG in partnership with global research firm Brandon Hall Group revealed that the top-ranked risk identified by participating organisations was "an insufficient pipeline of future leaders".[3]

In the same study, when asked how effective their current succession planning processes were, over 39% of these organisations responded that they either had no succession planning process or that their existing process was not at all effective. Furthermore, only 26% were of the opinion that their leadership succession planning was "extremely effective" or "very effective".[4]

Such research findings serve to highlight the basis for the prevailing crisis of confidence in leadership succession planning and management practices that has emerged in recent years. They are also symptomatic of a range of shortcomings associated with contemporary leadership succession programmes, most notably:

- Managing leadership succession in isolation.
- Failure to translate strategic priorities into future leadership capabilities.
- Reliance on performance as the sole predictor of future potential.
- Subjective and inconsistent definitions of potential.
- Reliance on generic leadership development programmes.
- Poor leader transition support.
- Lack of robust succession governance and oversight.

All of the above give rise to a range of succession-related risks, the most impactful of which include *inter alia* the risk of critical leadership positions remaining vacant for extended periods; appointed successors being ill-prepared to take on the responsibilities of their new roles; derailment as a result of poor on-boarding and assimilation into the new roles; and the misalignment of individual capabilities with position requirements.[5] If left unattended, such risks can have dire implications for the effectiveness of leadership successions, causing damage to careers; severely compromising the future supply of leadership talent; and ultimately, undermining organisational performance.

Against the above backdrop of prevailing crisis of confidence in leadership succession planning and management practices, the purpose of my chapter is to suggest how organisations can address the challenge of becoming future-fit in terms of their requisite leadership capability and capacity, considering both the demand for and supply of leadership talent, with the main emphasis on the latter. My chapter covers the following topics: The move in talent-savvy organisations towards a more proactive, strategically aligned leadership talent approach; understanding leadership talent demand in an increasingly dynamic context; defining leadership potential; predicting future potential in a VUCA world; [progress] towards a refined dimensional structure of leadership potential; and key considerations when identifying potential.

The Move in Talent-Savvy Organisations towards a More Proactive, Strategically Aligned Leadership Talent Approach

The challenge to organisations is to have the right leaders in the right numbers at the right time in the right place, able, willing, wanting, and being allowed to perform, thereby giving the organisation a sustainable competitive edge in its chosen markets. In response to this challenge, talent-savvy organisations are moving beyond the traditional replacement planning exercises to a more proactive, strategically aligned approach to succession planning and management. This necessitates that talent decisions should be more objective and evidence-based, with a strong emphasis on future-focused success criteria at all leadership levels. This represents a distinct departure from the more informal or "intuitive" nature of many talent decisions of the past.

A core component in this approach involves identifying the leadership talent that already exists in the organisation, in particular those individuals who have the potential for long-term future performance in roles beyond the next designated position in their career path. Succession management effectiveness therefore necessitates a focus across multiple time horizons, namely, the short- to medium-term matching of individuals to existing positions with known, position-specific "success profiles" and the longer-term prediction of individual potential to become eligible candidates – with the necessary support and development – for a range of possible future positions.[6]

Since the type of leadership required, and how it is defined, must reflect both the context in which it currently operates as well as the anticipated future contexts, the latter scenario is certainly more challenging than the former. Why? Primarily because both the individuals concerned and the future positions are likely to change over time before appointment is even considered. The magnitude of this challenge has increased exponentially over the past decade, given the unprecedented pace at which the world is changing.

Fundamental to the success of this approach to leadership succession optimisation by organisations aspiring to become talent-savvy is the acknowledgement of the systemic nature of the strategic talent management imperative and the incorporation of this principle into both the design and execution of such programmes. This is best achieved by recognising the positioning of leadership succession within the context of a broader talent management landscape, which provides the "conceptual framework and tools" informing strategic talent management within an organisational context.[7]

According to Veldsman, a talent management landscape is comprised of three interdependent dimensions, namely, the strategic talent management building blocks (the "what"), the process (the "how"), and the plan (the outcome as the "whereto"), resulting from the former two dimensions.[8] Figure 2.1 presents a talent management landscape depicting the interconnectivity and interrelatedness of the blocks building of strategic talent management.

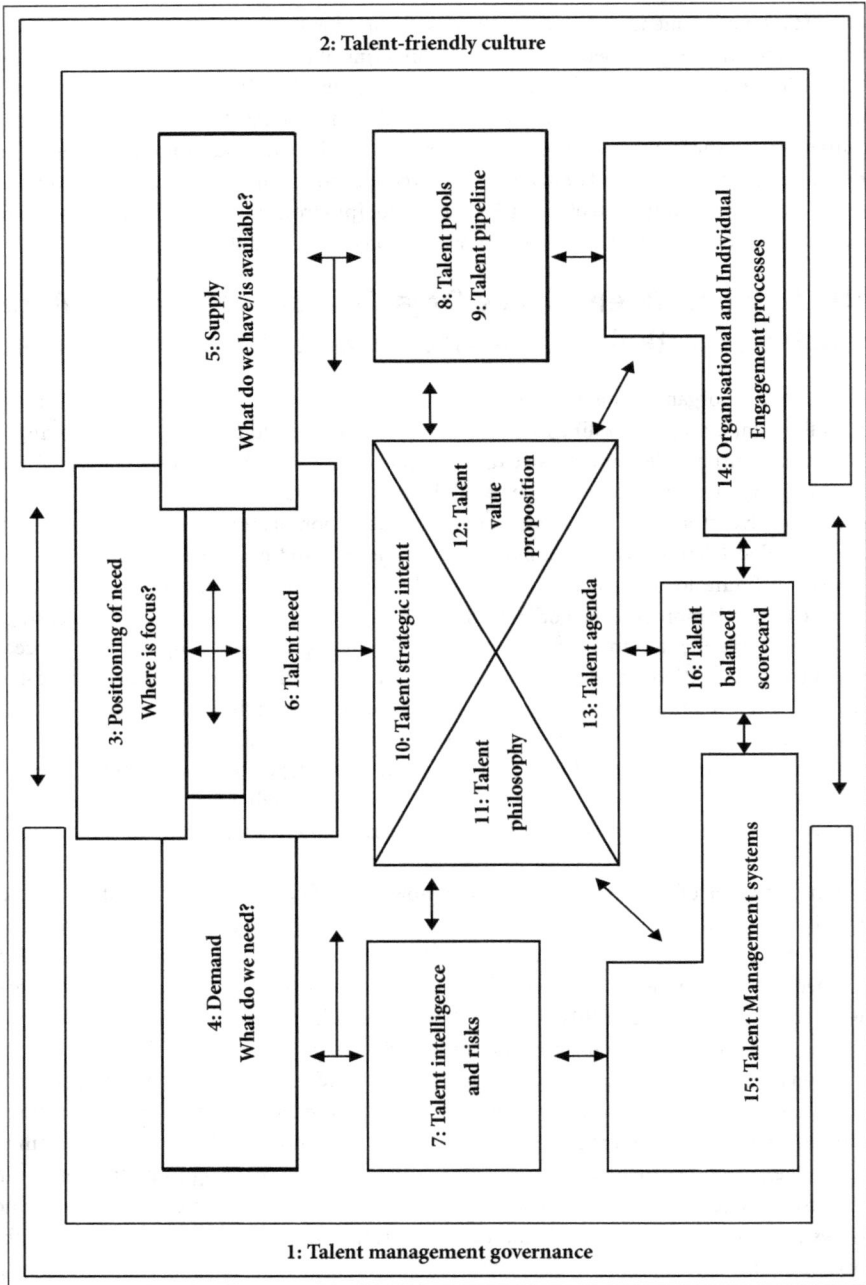

Figure 2.1: The building blocks comprising the talent management landscape
Source: *Veldsman, 2011*[9]

The strategic talent management process within an organisation involves the sequential execution of these building blocks, referred to by Veldsman as the "execution logic".[6] He argues that the numbering of the building blocks in Figure 2.1 reflects the most likely execution logic of addressing the building blocks as an organisation moves through the talent management landscape.[10]

While the primary focus of this chapter is on ensuring a sustainable supply of leadership talent for the future, Figure 2.1 clearly highlights the dependencies between this building block and those both preceding and following it. Systemic, integrated, strategic talent management is therefore imperative.

Addressing today's complex leadership succession challenges therefore calls for a new perspective, one involving a holistic and dynamic approach to identifying leadership potential that is strategically aligned, evidence-based, and contextually relevant. Though the primary focus of my chapter is on the supply of leadership talent, the demand side of leadership, which deals with context relevancy, also needs to receive some attention. Though not addressed, the demand for and supply of leadership talent management must be considered against the backdrop of the total talent management landscape, in this way adopting a strategic view of talent management.

Understanding Leadership Talent Demand in an Increasingly Dynamic Context

To remain relevant, leadership has to constantly adapt to, and align with, the prevailing context. By extension therefore, if the world is changing at an unprecedented pace, then the definition of what constitutes effective leadership has to change accordingly. In essence, the type of leadership required, and how it is defined, must reflect both the context in which it currently operates as well as anticipated future contexts that may emerge.

The careers of many of today's leaders have spanned periods of relative stability and predictability, and both the criteria and methods used to select, develop and promote them have reflected this reality. The consequence of this is that they are not suitably equipped to deal with the challenges of leading in a deeply disrupted context such as that which is being experienced globally right now.

The rate of change we are experiencing today is unprecedented, and differs significantly from that encountered in the past. It is occurring at a faster pace, lasting longer, and its impact is globally pervasive, causing broader and deeper disruption. This has resulted in the emergence of a new reality that is increasingly being referred to as a "VUCA" context, one which is challenging even the most capable of leaders, many of whom may be experiencing their skills becoming obsolete as their organisations transform. As a result, leadership agility and adaptability have emerged as essential skills if organisations are to survive and excel in this new reality. In a recent study, the Boston Consulting Group concluded that organisations today must shift their business models – and their leadership skills – to become "adaptive firms". These are firms which can adjust and learn more efficiently and effectively than their competitors, thus securing them an "adaptive advantage".[11]

Notwithstanding the widespread confirmation of the universal impact of this VUCA context on organisational leadership, the research underpinning the Development Dimensions International Global Leadership Forecast 2014/2015 revealed that less than two-thirds of leaders surveyed said they were either "highly confident" or "very confident" in their ability to meet the four VUCA challenges. This sentiment was mirrored by the HR professionals surveyed, slightly more than a third of whom considered their organisation's leaders as not capable of meeting these challenges. At best, only about 18% identified their leaders as "very capable".[12]

The extensive disruption inherent in today's business world has been described as the "new normal", and it is profoundly changing not only how organisations do business, but how business leaders lead. The skills and abilities leaders once needed to help their organisations thrive are no longer sufficient. A study conducted by Oxford Economics and Towers Watson suggests that leaders in 2021 must be comfortable "operating in a much more global environment, managing in the digital age, responding agilely and nimbly to economic, political and regulatory influences, and improving their ability to co-create, collaborate and team effectively with employees".[13]

Those accountable for leadership succession planning and management can help their organisations by selecting, developing and actively supporting the career progression of the leadership talent who not only demonstrate the skills, capabilities and behaviours to succeed in today's VUCA context, but perhaps more importantly, also possess the requisite potential to make the transition to positions of far greater scope and significance in an increasingly uncertain and deeply disrupted future.

Let us now move onto the supply side of leadership talent.

Defining Leadership Potential

The concept of high-potential talent is integral to the leadership succession planning and development process in most organisations today. A significant amount of time, effort and resources are invested into identifying, developing and retaining these individuals. However, the term "high potential" is often interpreted, defined and applied differently, both within and between organisations. This absence of a universally accepted definition of "high potential" understandably results in differences of opinion on who comprises the high-potential cohort.

According to Silzer and Church, the definition of high potential has evolved from an initial focus on past performance to being focused on the capability to handle specific known positions in the near-term future, and finally to predicting the capability to handle ill-defined long-term future roles, some of which may not yet exist.[14] Both the past performance and near-term-based definitions entail matching known persons to known positions. Both of these approaches are currently used in leadership succession planning and management programmes, particularly in stable organisations where there is limited change in organisational structures and roles. However, the former approach now typically constitutes a pre-condition to even be considered as a high potential.

The long-term definition requires organisations to identify the factors (or characteristics) that will predict success in a range of future leadership roles and operating contexts. This constitutes a much more difficult prediction challenge. Silzer and Church argue that it is this approach to defining high potential that talent management specialists need to master in order to provide their organisations with the assurance of a sustainable supply of future leaders.[15]

Predicting Future Potential in a VUCA World

The original approach has been the "names in boxes" replacement planning approach where individuals were pre-identified as the likely successors to incumbents in key positions. Over the past two decades leadership succession planning and management programmes have evolved and matured to the current practices which focus on the identification and development of talent for long-term organisational needs, which incorporate the use of sophisticated scenario-planning technology and predictive data-analytics. These more mature practices have enabled talent management specialists to refine their high potential talent initiatives in order to identify those individuals with the potential to succeed in positions well beyond their next planned career move. It is also important to identify these individuals earlier on in their careers.

In a dynamic VUCA context, traditional approaches to succession planning predicated on the notion of knowing which positions will need to be filled in the future – and which employees will be able to fill them – are likely to fall short of expectations. Instead, a more viable approach is to accept that uncertainty is a reality, and to identify ways to accommodate it. Accordingly, a number of organisations have introduced the concept of talent pools to mitigate the risk of uncertainty. This typically entails the identification of groups of high-potential individuals who are then developed for a range of potential roles, rather than for specific jobs which may or may not exist in the future. As and when vacancies do arise, those candidates from the talent pool who are regarded as the best fit will be considered for appointment.

Despite these significant advances, many leadership succession planning and management programmes continue to deliver suboptimal results. These results have largely been attributed to the inherent complexity of making predictions about the future long-term success of individuals designated as high potentials. In the prevailing VUCA context this prediction challenge becomes exponentially more complex, where future organisational strategies are unclear, markets are undergoing significant disruption, and organisational structures are constantly evolving.

Research by Martin and Schmidt on leadership succession transitions has revealed that nearly 40% of internal job moves made by people identified by their companies as high potentials end in failure.[16] Peters and Sevy (2014) point out that the Korn Ferry Institute, however, estimates that business leaders overrate the potential of their talent as much as 80% of the time.[17] Evidence of such high levels of misidentification of high-potential leaders should be cause for concern amongst those accountable for talent management. It must serve as a call to action to review their current leadership succession approaches, frameworks and associated practices.

Towards a Refined Dimensional Structure of Leadership Potential

The evolution of leadership succession planning and management approaches and programmes has been accompanied by an increase in the development of potential models.[18 19 20 21 22 23 24 25 26]

Following a review of these models, as well as a range of others in use at a number of organisations, Silzer and Church identified several key themes among the underlying components in the various models. Table 2.1 presents a summary of the themes.[27]

Table 2.1: Dominant themes across current models of potential cognitive abilities

	Conceptual or strategic thinking, breadth of thinking
	Intellect, cognitive ability
	Dealing with complexity/ambiguity
Personality variables	Interpersonal skills, sociability
	Dominance
	Maturity, stability, resilience
Learning variables	Adaptability, flexibility
	Learning orientation, interest in learning
	Openness to feedback

Leadership skills	Leadership capabilities, manage and empower people
	Developing others
	Influencing, inspiring, challenging the status quo, change management
Motivation variables	Drive, energy, engagement, tenacity
	Aspiration, drive for advancement, ambition, career drive, organizational commitment
	Results orientation, risk taking
Performance record	Performance track record
	Leadership experiences
Other variables	Technical/functional skills, business knowledge
	Qualifiers – for example, mobility, diversity
	Cultural fit

Source: *Silzer & Church*[28]

Despite the comprehensiveness of the list of themes identified, Silzer and Church question the practicality thereof for organisational use. Hence they propose an alternative means of organising these variables into a three-dimensional structure of potential that they believe offers greater utility.

Dimension 1: Foundational

The potential components are described as being consistent and remaining relatively stable across different contexts over time. Consequently, they are likely to measure close to the same level throughout an individual's career, and development of these components will be difficult. Examples include cognitive abilities and certain personality variables.[29]

Dimension 2: Growth

Silzer and Church consider these components to be enablers or inhibitors of an individual's growth and development. They classify them as "intervening variables" to learning, which can serve as indicators of whether an individual will develop further and learn new skills. Similarly to their opinion of the foundational components , they regard these components as being consistent and stable across situations. What differentiates these components in their view is the level to which they may be more or less evident, depending on a combination of an individual's level of interest in a particular area, and the available opportunity and support to learn more in that area of interest. Examples of these components are adaptability and learning orientation.[30]

Dimension 3: Career

These components of potential are regarded as "early indicators" of the skill sets required in specific careers, and Silzer and Church believe that they are therefore career path specific.

Furthermore, they contend that the extent to which these components can be learned and developed depends on the presence of the growth components and the level of support afforded by the work setting.[31]

A categorisation by Silzer and Church of the summary themes contained in Table 2.1 according to these three types of potential dimensions is presented in Table 2.2.

Table 2.2: Proposed dimensional structure of potential

Foundational Dimension	
Cognitive	Conceptual or strategic thinking, breadth of thinking
	Intellect, cognitive ability
	Dealing with complexity/ambiguity.
Personality	Interpersonal skills, sociability
	Dominance
	Maturity, emotional stability, resilience
Growth Dimension	
Learning	Adaptability, flexibility
	Learning orientation, interest in learning
	Openness to feedback
Motivation	Drive, energy, engagement, tenacity
	Aspiration, drive for advancement, ambition, career drive, organisational commitment
	Results orientation, risk taking
Career Dimension	
Leadership skills	Leadership capabilities, manage and empower people (general)
	Developing others
	Influencing, inspiring, challenging the status quo, change management
Performance record	Performance track record (career relevant)
	Career experiences
Other variables	Technical/functional skills, business knowledge
	Qualifiers: for example mobility, diversity
	Cultural fit: Career relevant values and norms

Source: *Silzer & Church, 2009*[32]

According to Silzer and Church. this proposed dimensional structure suggests that potential may comprise both common generic components and career-specific components. The Foundational and Growth dimensions serve as predictors of potential for a broad range of careers. The career dimensions are relevant to only certain career paths.[33] They see the common components of potential and career potential respectively as follows:

- **Common components of potential**
  o Foundational dimension – Cognitive and Personality variables
  o Growth dimension – Learning and Motivation variables
- **Career-specific components of potential**
  o Career dimension – Leadership, Performance, Technical/Functional variables

Key Considerations when Identifying Potential

In their endeavours to bolster leadership bench-strength at all levels, an increasing number of organisations are striving to identify high-potential future leaders earlier in their careers. Given the nature of the three categories of potential proposed by Silzer and Church, this requires consideration of two important factors:

- The stage in an individual's career when it becomes feasible to predict long-term potential; and
- Whether different components of potential become more or less predictive of long-term potential at different stages during an individual's career.[34]

The consistency and stability of the Foundational dimension suggests that they can be identified at any career stage using a combination of consistent metrics. Since the Career dimension is likely to evolve over the duration of an individual's career, in contrast, identification should be undertaken using only career stage-relevant metrics.

It is the opinion of Silzer and Church that certain of the components underlying the Growth dimension – for example, adaptability and achievement orientation – can be identified using similar metrics at different career stages. Other components are more contextually dependent, for example, career ambition and learning orientation. Their identification may necessitate that individuals have the opportunity to be deployed across a range of roles to see if these previously latent components emerge.[35]

The Design of a Potential Identification Process

For organisations seeking to ensure a sustainable supply of future leaders at all levels, it is certainly worthwhile considering the design of a potential identification process that proceeds sequentially through the approach advocated by Silzer and Church.[36]

Step 1: Identify foundational dimensions

The first step should focus on the identification of the more stable and consistent cognitive and personality based components of the Foundational dimension of potential. There is a range of standardised assessment instruments currently available in the market which has proved to be the most effective and efficient means of serving this purpose.

Step 2: Identify stable and context-dependent growth dimensions

The second step would essentially involve two phases, the first being the identification of the stable components underlying the Growth dimension. The second is the identification of those components which may be latent owing to current roles and/or operating contexts.

The identification of potential on the Growth dimension is critical, because the outcome will have significant implications for decisions concerning investment in future development and learning initiatives. Moreover, should an individual demonstrate low potential on this dimension, it is unlikely that they will demonstrate high potential on the leadership Career path specific dimension, which would limit their long-term potential to acquire the skill and abilities required for success in future leadership roles.[37]

Step 3: Identify stage-appropriate career dimensions

Once it has been confirmed that an individual possesses potential in both the Foundational and Growth dimensions, it then becomes necessary to measure them against career path or career stage specific success profiles. The outcome of this process will equip an organisation to design and deliver personalised career-path and career-stage specific development experiences to enable the individuals concerned to realise their identified long-term potential.

The three-dimensional structure proposed by Silzer and Church provides an innovative perspective on the nature of potential and how it can be identified in individuals.

Conclusion

Assuring a sustainable supply of leaders at all levels has become a key imperative for organisations globally. However, evidence emerging from research undertaken by leading consulting firms suggests that these same organisations are struggling to identify and develop a pipeline of effective leaders who are capable of tackling long-term strategic challenges in a "VUCA" context.[38] [39] [40] It is becoming apparent with increasing regularity that traditional methods used to select and develop talent have not kept pace with the changing requirements for effective leadership, and are thus failing to deliver on expectations.

In the past, when markets were more predictable and organisational structures and roles were stable, it made sense to assess candidates for high-potential programmes based on their performance track record and measure them against current known leadership success profiles. However, in an operating context where disruption has become the norm, where strategies are rendered obsolete with increasing frequency, and where future leadership positions may not yet exist, such an approach is no longer valid.

Instead, it has become essential to understand an individual's potential to handle the rapidly changing and often volatile nature of today's business context, and their capability to grow into increasingly expansive, complex and unknown leadership roles. The three-dimensional structure of potential proposed by Silzer and Church, and the related approach to identifying potential across the underlying component variables across different career stages and contexts, provides a viable point of departure to address this challenge.

Notwithstanding the benefits to be derived from a more robust approach to identifying long-term leadership potential, it must be borne in mind that the analysis of potential constitutes a single, albeit keystone, element in an integrated strategic talent-management landscape.[41] Failure to acknowledge and incorporate this into the design and execution of a leadership succession planning and management strategy is likely to yield a compromised leadership pipeline, containing leaders who lack the requisite capability to deal with the complexities of the emerging VUCA reality.

In contrast, doing so effectively, by fully leveraging the interdependencies of the elements comprising the talent management landscape, will yield a sustainable supply of future leaders ready to take full advantage of a combination of holistic, individualised and blended development experiences focused on personal and professional learning and growth opportunities that are aligned with anticipated strategic priorities in an increasingly dynamic context.

Endnotes

1	Deloitte, 2016.	22	Hewitt Associates, 2008, in
2	Development Dimensions International, 2014.		Silzer & Church, 2009.
3	KPMG, 2013.	23	Hogan Assessment Systems, 2009,
4	KPMG, 2013.		in Silzer & Church, 2009.
5	Corporate Leadership Council, 2003.	24	McCall, 1998.
6	Silzer & Church, 2009.	25	Peterson & Erdahl, 2007.
7	Veldsman, 2011.	26	Rowe, 2007.
8	Veldsman, 2011.	27	Silzer & Church, 2009.
9	Veldsman, 2011, p. 368.	28	Silzer & Church, 2009.
10	Veldsman, 2011.	29	Silzer & Church, 2009.
11	Reeves & Love, 2012.	30	Silzer & Church, 2009.
12	Development Dimensions International, 2014.	31	Silzer & Church, 2009.
13	Oxford Economics, 2012.	32	Silzer & Church, 2009.
14	Silzer & Church, 2009.	33	Silzer & Church, 2009.
15	Silzer & Church, 2009.	34	Silzer & Church, 2009.
16	Martin & Schmidt, 2010.	35	Silzer & Church, 2009.
17	Peters & Sevy, 2014.	36	Silzer & Church, 2009.
18	Barnett, 2008.	37	Silzer & Church, 2009.
19	Corporate Leadership Council, 2005.	38	Deloitte, 2016.
20	Rogers & Smith, 2007.	39	Development Dimensions International, 2014.
21	Hay Group, 2008, in Silzer & Church, 2009.	40	KPMG, 2013.
		41	Veldsman, 2011.

References

Barnett, R. 2008. *Identifying high potential talent*. Minneapolis, MN: MDA Leadership Consulting, Inc.

Corporate Leadership Council. 2003. *Assessment methods for identifying leadership potential*. Washington, DC: Corporate Executive Board.

Corporate Leadership Council. 2005. *Realizing the full potential of rising talent (Volume I): A Quantitative analysis of the identification and development of high potential employees*. Washington, DC: Corporate Executive Board.

Deloitte. 2016. *Global human capital trends 2016. The new organization: Different by design*. Westlake, TX: Deloitte University Press.

Development Dimensions International. 2014. *Global leadership forecast 2014/2015. Ready-now leaders: Meeting tomorrow's business challenges*. Bridgeville, PA: Development Dimensions International.

Hay Group. 2008. *Growth factor index (GFI): Technical manual*. ([Online]. Available: http://www.haygroup. com). [Accessed 11 August 2016].

Hewitt Associates. 2008. *Getting to high potential: How organizations define and calibrate their critical talent*. Hewitt Associates [Online]. Available: http://www.hewitt.com. [Accessed 11 August 2016].

Hogan Assessment Systems. 2009. *Sample high potential, candidate assessment report*. Tulsa, OK: Hogan Assessment Systems [Online]. Available: http://www.hoganassessments.com. [Accessed 11 August 2016].

KPMG. 2013. *Time for a More Holistic Approach to Talent Risk*. KPMG International.

Martin, J & Schmidt, C. 2010. 'How to Keep Your Top Talent'. *Harvard Business Review* 88(5):54–61.

McCall, M W, Jr. 1998. *High Flyers: Developing the Next Generation of Leaders*. Boston, MA: Harvard Business School Press.

Oxford Economics. 2012. *Global Talent 2021: How the New Geography of Talent Will Transform Human Resources Strategies*. Oxford, UK: Oxford Economics.

Peters, J & Sevy, B. 2014. *The High Cost of Misidentifying High-Potential Leaders*. Los Angeles, CA: The Korn Ferry Institute.

Peterson, DB & Erdahl, P. 2007. *Early Identification and Development of Senior Leadership Talent: The Secret Insider's Guide*. Workshop presented at the Annual conference of the Society of Industrial-Organizational Psychology, New York, April, 2007.

Reeves, M & Love, C. 2012. 'The Most Adaptive Companies 2012: Winning in an Age of Turbulence'. *Bcg. perspectives*, 21 August. Boston, MA: Boston Consulting Group (BCG). Viewed [Accessed 1 July 2016], from https://www.bcgperspectives.com/content/articles/corporate_strategy_portfolio_management_future_of_strategy_most_adaptive_companies_2012/

Rogers, RW & Smith, AB. 2007. *Finding Future Perfect Senior Leaders: Spotting Executive Potential*. Bridgeville, PA: Development Dimensions International.

Rowe, K. 2007. How to Identify Leadership Potential. *UK Guide to Skills and Learning*, 234–236.

Silzer, R & Church, A. 2009. 'The Pearls and Perils of Identifying Potential'. *Industrial and Organizational Psychology* 2(4):377–412.

Veldsman, TH. 2011. 'Crafting and Implementing Integrated Talent Management in Pursuit of Sustainable Talent Excellence', in I Boninelli & T Meyer (eds). *Human Capital Trends: Building a Sustainable Organisation*. Johannesburg, South Africa: Knowledge Resources, pp. 359–390.

SECTION 3

LEADERSHIP ASSESSMENT AND DEVELOPMENT

Chapter 3

LEADERSHIP ASSESSMENT

Nicola Taylor and Paul Vorster

According to Deloitte's 2014 *Global Human Capital Trends* survey, the most urgent trend in organisations has to do with building global leadership. This need is the same for all job levels, geographies and functional areas, but the strongest focus is on traditional leadership in senior management positions.[1] Development Dimensions International's 2015 Global Leadership Survey[2] identifies key actions for the preparation and development of leaders to allow them to deal effectively with future challenges. In both these reports, leadership development is considered a key element for the survival and continued growth of organisations.

What is interesting is that there is no consensus on a single definition of what a leader is, what they should look like, or specifically what makes them successful, which makes identifying them very tricky.[3] However, we do know that leadership relates to broader aspects of performance and effectiveness within the organisation. For example, leadership and effectiveness have been shown to relate to employee and subordinate performance,[4] employee retention,[5] general organisational effectiveness, and organisational citizenship performance.[6]

You would have been exposed all kinds of leadership in the preceding chapters: servant leadership, moral leadership, ethical leadership, transformational leadership, democratic leadership, and primal leadership, to name but a few. These different types of leadership place an emphasis on a different leadership characteristic. That is not to say that numerous styles of leadership are not important, but it is next to impossible for a single leader to display all of these various styles of leadership at one time. What is important is to have the right style of leadership to match the needs of the organisation.[7]

Currently one of the greatest challenges that leaders face is dealing with a VUCA context: A volatile, uncertain, complex and ambiguous world. If organisations and their leaders are unable to operate effectively in this kind of context, associated with the rapid changes that globalisation and technology have introduced, they will be unable to ensure that their organisations stay competitive. Only 25% of organisations surveyed in 2014 felt that their leaders were VUCA-capable.[8] There is thus a massive need to ensure that the right leaders are in the right place at the right time.

Prospective leaders generally have to run the leadership pipeline gauntlet in order to reach the top positions in organisations.[9] This pipeline usually has formal (for example, psychometric measurement, assessment centres, structured interviews) and informal (for example, performance on the job, unstructured interviews, opportunities) selection and exclusion processes that deter individuals with little leadership capability and promote potential leaders up the ranks in the organisation. This gauntlet tests the prospective leader in numerous ways, and the process separates the chaff (= non-leaders) from the wheat (= leaders), so to speak.

Ultimately, leaders in top positions did not just get there by accident but had to demonstrate specific skills, knowledge, attributes, competencies, traits, and aptitudes to enter leadership positions.[10] Therefore, studying the characteristics of effective leaders can illuminate what the "right stuff" may be for leadership in organisations. Using psychometric assessments provides an objective source of information to add to the pile when considering an individual's natural propensity for taking on leadership positions. This chapter looks at when organisations should include psychometric assessment for leadership, what types of instruments are generally used, and the constructs that should be considered when assessing leaders.

When Do We Assess?

Depending on the need, psychometric instruments can be used at any point in the leadership pipeline, as well as at any point in the human resources processes. The role that the instruments will play may be different at each stage, but a properly integrated assessment strategy can make the best use of psychometric instruments in the most cost-effective way.

For example, once you have identified the key psychological constructs required for the leadership position, you would create your battery of instruments and apply the battery in the recruitment or selection process. Once you have your ideal candidate, you can use those same psychometric instruments in the "on-boarding" process to help the leader understand the organisation and how he/she fits in. The results of the psychometric instruments can be used in the leader's personal development plan, to help the leader understand how he/she fits with members of the team or organisation, and to develop the skills the leader may need in the future. At a later stage, the leader can be reassessed to evaluate whether he or she has changed or developed over time. This information can then be used to 'fine-tune' the leader's development plan.

The key to using psychometric assessments for leadership selection and development (or for any purpose in the organisation, for that matter) is balance. It is important not to create "assessment fatigue" in the organisation, but to make the best use of psychometric assessments to harness skills and create concrete development plans. Some organisations have departments that create surveys to measure anything and everything, to the extent that the perceived value of the survey results becomes watered-down and diminished. By the same token, under-assessing will mean that too much emphasis is placed on one or two constructs, to the extent that their value is overemphasised and sometimes stretched past the actual scope of the assessment results. With this in mind, regular assessment audits are vital to ensure that the right psychometric instruments are being used at the right time, for the right people, and for the right purpose.

Another aspect that needs to be taken into account when using psychometrics for leadership selection and development is the level of "test-readiness" of the organisation. Some organisations use objective testing information to make hiring, staffing, and development decisions. Others simply use this process as a veneer, or not at all. If an organisation implements an expensive psychometric testing process, but does not use the results effectively, psychometric testing may not be a process that adds any value to the organisation. This is especially true if psychometric test results are ignored, side-lined, or have very little relation to the leadership constructs deemed important for the leadership role. Organisations therefore have to understand first why they are using psychometric instruments to measure leadership constructs, and how this information will be used to make decisions about leadership selection, development and succession processes.

In deciding if, when, and where to implement psychometric testing processes, organisations need to consider the following four key aspects of their current and future use of psychometric testing:

- Whether the psychometric test results will be used to make high-stakes decisions about employees in the organisation;
- Whether the objective test results will be used as a primary indicator of leadership potential or whether there are other more important sources of information that should be used;
- Whether individuals in the organisation that make hiring and staff decisions use the results of the psychometric testing in their staffing decisions or not; and
- Whether the psychometric tests being used are related to the psychological constructs that were identified as important by using a job-analysis process.

There are also other elements the organisation must have considered at length before using psychometric testing. These may include: (i) the format of testing (for example, computer-based, adaptive, group-testing, individual-testing, online testing, paper-and-pencil testing); (ii) who may administer the psychometric instrument (in other words, scope of practice); (iii) fairness, validity and reliability of the tests used in the organisation; and (iv) how the results of the psychometric tests will be used. There are various laws and regulations in different countries regarding the use of psychometric assessments. Practitioners and organisations should be well-acquainted with those relevant in their country if they plan on implementing psychometric testing in the organisation.

How Do We Assess?

There are a number of different ways through which information can be obtained using assessments. It is important to understand that "how" people are assessed is as important – if not more so – than "what" is assessed, or "who" is assessed. Generally, there are four main methods of assessment that are used either independently, or combined in certain ways to obtain assessment information. Firstly, practitioner one-on-one assessment is used when the constructs being measured are high stakes and require some form of observation (in other words, intelligence and clinical testing). Self-report inventories, which are very popular, are often administered without direct supervision and are thus geared towards online or group testing. This makes these instruments very cost effective, but may also open them up to faking responses.

Sometimes assessment happens through pure observation only. This is often the case with assessment centres, where a rater observes individuals and then rates them on the construct of interest. This technique eliminates faking, but can be somewhat subjective. More recently, 360-degree inventories have become a popular method of assessment. This is because these instruments have the advantages of a self-report, but then verify this information by asking other people who know the test-taker to rate the test-taker on behavioural criteria as well. The 360-degree technique therefore helps to eliminate faking or impression management and also provides insight into how others perceive the individual. In the following sections we will discuss some of these methods of assessment together with their advantages and disadvantages.

Practitioner one-on-one administration

Some psychometric instruments require the practitioner to administer a test or process to an individual in a one-on-one setting. These "tests" or "assessments" are usually done to obtain an indication of cognitive ability or intelligence, level of complexity, or where narrative information is important to the psychological assessment. This mode of administration allows the practitioner to observe the person making the responses, which provides a much more in-depth analysis of the person's behaviour.

Interviews may also fall under this heading, but one needs to be very careful when using interviews for decision-making. Behaviour-based structured interviews are deemed to be the best kind, as they are legally and psychometrically more easily defensible.[11] Each person is given the same questions, which are relevant to the job requirements. The types of questions asked in interviews may be hypothetical, situational or causal, and are used to elicit examples of relevant workplace behaviour.

Self-report questionnaires

One of the most popular methods of psychometric assessment is the self-report questionnaire. It is quick and easy to administer, usually electronically, with feedback reports available immediately. There is some concern from practitioners about the validity of self-report questionnaires in leadership assessment.[12] Some practitioners worry that they are easily manipulated, fairly transparent (it is easy to determine what they measure when completing them), and subject to bias from response styles (certain groups of people respond in a specific manner, or consistently score lower/higher than another group). The concern is therefore that self-report inventories do not provide an accurate picture of the individual being assessed. While it is true that factors such as self-awareness, state of mind, and motivation may have an impact on the accuracy of the self-report responses, self-report test results are still demonstrably valid, reliable, and allow for consistent prediction of important behavioural outcomes in the workplace despite these perceived shortcomings.[13] The effect of 'faking', where the candidate purposefully misrepresents themselves when completing a self-report, is also deemed to have little practical impact on the accuracy of test results.[14]

Assessment centre/observation

The use of simulation exercises in what is known as assessment centres (or development centres) has a long, rich history. Many started around the time of the Second World War, where personnel selection became critical, along with the identification of officer potential, halting the reliance on social hierarchy for officer selection.[15] There has been growth in the popularity of assessment centres as a decision-making tool within organisations, but it is important to state what we mean when we refer to these centres.

An assessment centre essentially is an event. However, we can also consider it to be an approach to obtaining a wide range of information about a person. We can describe assessment centres as a process of assessment that may include psychometric instruments to complement assessment centre activities. Usually, assessment centres consist of a one- or two-day process where the individual participates in a number of activities (called simulation exercises) that are designed to elicit behaviours that would be displayed in the workplace. Individual performance during these assessment centre activities is then rated by observers according to behavioural or functional competency checklists.

Assessment centres are important for job-performance prediction,[16] as they allow a close simulation of the activities the person will be expected to perform. The types of activities generally include:

- **In-baskets:** dealing with standard on-the-job emails and memos that need to be prioritised and dealt with systematically;
- **Case studies:** responding to a particular work situation or dilemma;
- **Role plays:** interacting with a person posing as a client or colleague;
- **Presentations:** presenting to a panel on a job-specific topic; and
- **Various group activities:** for example, leaderless group discussions.

Many organisations choose to develop their own specific exercises, but there are also generic assessment centre solutions available for various roles.

360-degree assessment

The 360-degree assessment is a popular method of obtaining information about leaders. Many organisations use these instruments as part of their performance management system. In this instance, the individual is rated on critical job indicators by his/her manager, peers, and direct reports. These can be on psychological characteristics, such as personality or emotional intelligence, or on competencies related to the job or leadership role. Usually the individual also rates him-/herself, and the comparison between self-reported scores and those scores given by others can provide valuable self-insight that is not available from a self-report alone.

Although the relationships between ratings of peers, direct reports, and supervisors (so-called *other ratings*) on particular competency dimensions and personality characteristics appear weak to moderate in the literature, this has not stopped researchers from treating such relationships as important.[17] In fact, a meta-analysis of 263 individual samples and over 44 178 cases indicate that *other ratings* of human behaviour have incremental validity beyond *self-reported* behaviour, and thus facilitate a more complete understanding of an individual's behavioural tendencies and make-up.[18] 360-degree assessment also acts as a check-and-balance for some of the perceived shortcomings of self-report questionnaires because the individual's self-reported data is moderated by others.

What Do We Assess?

The differential psychology approach to leadership searches for those constructs that make leaders effective or different from those who do not lead, or are not effective in organisations. These leadership constructs relate to more than just inherent human traits; they also relate to skills, attitudes and aptitudes.[19] Over the years a number of constructs have been identified that relate directly and indirectly to leadership effectiveness and work-performance. Kirkpatrick and Locke[20] identified the following constructs that leaders have that others do not: *Drive* (a need to achieve and compete); *leadership motivation* (the motivation to take charge and be responsible for others); *honesty and integrity; self-confidence; good cognitive ability; knowledge of the business; charisma*; and *creativity*.

Interestingly, Bass[21] identified very similar leadership constructs for the transformational leadership style such as:

- **Charisma:** the leader instils pride and belief in projects, tasks, and innovation;
- **Individualised consideration:** leader develops and takes into consideration subordinates;
- **Intellectual stimulation:** the leader challenges his/her followers intellectually;
- **Contingent reward:** the leader rewards performance; and
- **Management-by-exception:** the leader avoids micromanagement of subordinates and allows them to learn and develop independently.

A study of 127 456 executives in leadership positions found the following aspects common to all these leaders: Physical vitality and stamina; intelligence and action-orientated judgment; eagerness to accept responsibility; task competence; understanding the needs of followers; skill in dealing with people; a strong need for achievement; a capacity to motivate people; courage and resolution; decisiveness; self-confidence; assertiveness; and the ability to be adaptable and flexible.[22]

In a more recent meta-analysis, five primary dimensions of leadership have been proposed.[23] These five dimensions include:

- *Personal effectiveness:* being competent and organised;
- *Managerial effectiveness:* the ability to delegate to and monitor the performance of others;
- *Interpersonal relationship effectiveness:* the ability to get along with and motivate others;
- *Operational effectiveness:* being able to manage the task processes in organisations effectively; and
- *Societal effectiveness:* the realisation that external stakeholders outside the organisations must be taken into account when making decisions.

Leadership therefore appears to be a broad, complex and multifaceted phenomenon.[24] It also appears that there are a number of different, but overlapping, perspectives on what makes a leader effective. Although these constructs give us an indication of what is required in leadership positions they are not easily measurable. How would one measure flexibility, charisma, or self-confidence for example? Luckily, differential psychology has demonstrated that a number of leadership constructs can be measured and integrated.[25] These constructs and construct taxonomies include the following five broad domains: (i) behavioural tendencies and styles;[26] (ii) capabilities;[27] (iii) emotional make-up;[28] (iv) personal values and value orientations;[29] and (v) derailers.[30] Figure 3.1 depicts these graphically.

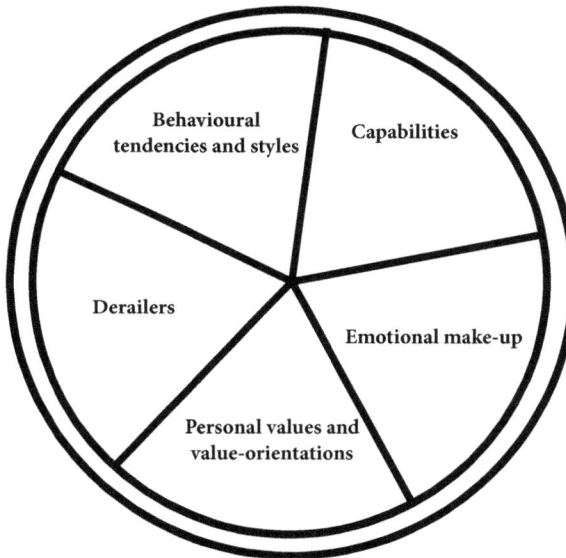

Figure 3.1: Common construct domains measured for leadership selection and development

Although a number of other constructs also exist for the measurement of leadership effectiveness, these broad domains cover a large proportion of measurable leadership attributes. We discuss the measurement of these five broad leadership construct domains in the next sections.

Behavioural tendencies and styles

One of the most common behavioural tendencies measured for leadership effectiveness comes from the personality psychology domain. Ultimately, behavioural tendencies and styles refer to the individual's day-to-day behaviour.[31]

Unfortunately, there is little consensus about the traits and attributes that make leaders effective.[32] The literature is so varied that some differential psychologists such as Judge et al. (2002) use the five-factor model of personality as a "leadership taxonomy" instead of qualitatively combining literature on leader behavioural attributes.

The five-factor model of personality is composed of Extraversion, Neuroticism (= Emotional Stability), Conscientiousness, Openness to Experience, and Agreeableness, which evidence suggests are universally applicable across numerous nationalities and cultures.[33] Generally, leadership research findings indicate that leaders have lower levels of Neuroticism, higher levels of Extraversion, higher levels of Openness to Experience, lower levels of Agreeableness, and higher Conscientiousness than non-leaders (Judge et al., 2002).[34] We briefly discuss the relationships these constructs have with leadership effectiveness below.

Neuroticism

Neuroticism has to do with a person's level of emotional stability and their experience of negative affect in the form of anxiety, depression, self-consciousness, guilt, anger, hostility and other similar emotions. Generally lower levels of Neuroticism are required for effective leadership performance.[35] This is because individuals who score higher on Neuroticism tend to have lower self-esteem, higher levels of anxiety, and lower levels of stress tolerance, which are not well-suited to leadership positions.[36] The most important and predictive element within Neuroticism appears to be self-esteem or self-confidence.[37] Having a high self-esteem, or positive self-concept, is critical for leadership effectiveness. It is difficult to get people to believe in you as a leader if you do not believe in yourself.

Extraversion

Extraversion is the tendency to be sociable and gregarious in groups, dominant, affiliation-seeking and sensation-seeking. Extraversion does not appear to be strongly predictive of leadership emergence or effectiveness in all situations.[38] However, Extraversion does tend to be related to "leader-like" behaviours or the tendency to seem or appear like a leader.[39] Generally, extraverted leaders are perceived to be energetic, lively, socially interactive, communicative, domineering, and restless.[40] Although these elements seem as though they should be related to leadership effectiveness, the literature indicates that they are only weakly related, with numerous studies reporting conflicting results.

Openness to experience

Openness to Experience (or Openness) is related to creativity, divergent thinking, curiosity and innovation.[41] Generally, higher levels of openness result in greater leadership effectiveness.[42] More specifically, creativity, a facet (or sub-factor) of Openness, appears to be the most predictive of leadership effectiveness. This is possibly due to the visionary nature of individuals with high levels of creativity.

Agreeableness

The relationship between Agreeableness and leadership effectiveness appears ambiguous in the literature. This is because some level of affiliation and interpersonal sensitivity (facets of Agreeableness) are required for effective leadership performance (= being rewarding to work with), but these constructs can also negate leadership effectiveness in very high amounts. For example, this can occur when the leader is so sensitive that he/she is unable to give authentic feedback to subordinates or stand up for what they believe in.[43] Because lower levels of Agreeableness are related to forthright feedback to peers, subordinates, and superiors, the affiliation component of Agreeableness appears to be negatively related to leadership effectiveness.

Conscientiousness

Conscientiousness refers to the tendency to pay attention to details, follow rules, delay gratification, persevere, and avoid risk. It is highly predictive of job-performance.[44] It also appears to relate positively to leadership effectiveness.[45] This is most likely due to the perseverance component of Conscientiousness, where leaders have to overcome, persevere, and follow through with tasks and projects in order to succeed. More importantly, high Conscientiousness also relates to a leader's propensity to pay attention to details and avoid unnecessary risk.

Capabilities

Capabilities refer to a broad taxonomy of skills, abilities, aptitudes, and cognition that leaders may need to be effective in their roles. Although specific aptitudes and skills are required for effective leadership, one of the most researched "capabilities" is the construct of intelligence.[46] Although intelligence is predictive of job-performance, it appears to be less predictive of leadership effectiveness than previously thought. Interestingly, intelligence was not strongly predictive of objective leadership performance criteria, although it was strongly related to perceptions of leadership effectiveness and leader emergence. This indicates that intelligent leaders are perceived to be more effective leaders although objectively they may not be.

Other constructs such as intellectual styles[47] have also been postulated to result in greater leadership effectiveness. Unfortunately, most studies investigating intellectual styles and leadership effectiveness have conflicting and ambiguous results. However, what is known is that certain intellectual styles appear to be conducive to upward mobility into leadership positions and are predictive of job-performance ratings. This is most likely because certain leaders with specific intellectual styles select other leaders who have similar intellectual styles to themselves to fill leadership positions.[48]

The idea is that like selects like, and intellectual styles are quite predictive of upward mobility into these leadership positions but not necessarily of leadership effectiveness. Further evidence also suggests that intellectual styles are related to cognitive complexity, which is defined as the capacity to deal effectively with informational complexity in order to make quality decisions and solve problems in the organisation. Intellectual styles are considered different from intelligence because they measure "how an individual uses his/her intelligence dynamically". Thus, intellectual styles measure constructs that intersect between behavioural tendencies, emotional make-up, personal value orientations, and intelligence. Intellectual styles therefore evaluate how well individuals are capable of functioning at high levels within the organisation.

Emotional make-up

The emotional make-up of leaders has been an area of great debate.[49] This is specifically true of emotional intelligence, which has been a popular construct in leadership selection and development.[50] It is important to realise that three primary models of emotional intelligence are available, namely trait-based emotional intelligence, ability-based emotional intelligence, and mixed-model emotional intelligence.[51]

Ability-based emotional intelligence has been found to be quite strongly related to indicators of leadership effectiveness, with experiential emotional intelligence (learned emotional intelligence) being the most predictive. Similarly, ability-based emotional intelligence tends to be moderately to strongly predictive of performance in executives in leadership roles, even when controlling for intelligence and personality.[52] Trait-based emotional intelligence is also predictive of organisational outcomes, but the literature is inconclusive as to whether it adds predictive value over and above personality. This suggests that elements within personality, such as Neuroticism and Agreeableness, also provide a good indication of the emotional make-up of leaders. However, the practical value those practitioners find in being able to approach emotional intelligence from a developmental perspective make it a useful addition to any leadership development battery.

Personal values and value-orientations

Although personal values and value-orientations are considered important for the organisational fit of employees,[53] very little research has been done on the relationship between personal values and value-orientations and their relationship with leadership effectiveness. Some research shows that value-orientations are related to leader performance in the military.[54] Interestingly, these value-orientations were related to the primary values of the military unit in which the study was conducted. This indicates that values are an important consideration when "fitting" leaders to organisations. Ultimately, values and value-orientations of leaders need to be congruent with the values of the organisation in which they operate for leadership effectiveness.

Additionally, Kirkpatrick and Locke[55] identified honesty and integrity as an important leadership value for leadership effectiveness in organisations. Unfortunately, integrity is generally a poorly defined construct in the literature. There are many assessment measures that purport to measure integrity, but actually measure certain counterproductive work behaviours. The main question that needs to be asked in this regard is whether the propensity for counterproductive work behaviours is due to certain personal values (in other words, risk taking), or due to poor individual–organisational value fit.

Derailers

Another popular construct or set of constructs measured for leadership effectiveness is derailer behaviour. A derailer is a blanket-term used to describe elements of intra- and interpersonal behaviours that may negate effectiveness on the job, or may damage the interpersonal relationships of employees in the work environment.[56] Usually, derailment is related to negative emotional states which may result in incorrect attributions of behaviour, or inappropriate behaviour in general. The measurement of derailers has become especially popular in executive level selection because these high-profile positions have an impact on most, if not all, functional areas in the organisation. Derailment behaviours in top positions can therefore be extremely damaging to the individual as well as the organisation.

Generally, derailers are negatively related to the managerial performance of leaders, especially with regard to trust, positive attitude, leading and decision-making. More specifically, passive aggression, emotional volatility, over-caution in decision-making, interpersonal avoidance, and a lack of reality checking before making decisions tend to be the most prevalent and damaging in leadership positions.[57]

Table 3.1: Examples of assessment instruments across the five domains

Behavioural tendencies and styles	California Psychological Inventory (CPI) Hogan Personality Inventory (HPI) Myers-Briggs Type Indicator (MBTI) NEO Personality Inventory (NEO-PI) Occupational Personality Questionnaire (OPQ) Sixteen Personality Factor Questionnaire (16PF) Work Personality Index (WPI)
Capabilities	Cognitive Process Profile (CPP) Career Path Appreciation (CPA) Complexity Navigation Test (CNT) Hogan Business Reasoning Inventory (HBRI) Learning Potential Computerized Adaptive Test (LPCAT) Raven's Progressive Matrices Wechsler Adult Intelligence Scales (WAIS)
Emotional make-up	Emotional Quotient Inventory 2.0 (EQ 2.0) Emotional and Social Competence Inventory (ESCI) Genos Emotional Intelligence Inventory (Genos EI) Mayer-Salovey Caruso Emotional Intelligence Test (MSCEIT) Trait Emotional Intelligence Questionnaire (TEIQue)
Personal values and value orientations	Career Values Scale (CVS) Motives, Values, Preferences Inventory (MVPI) Personal Globe Inventory (PGI) Self-Directed Search (SDS) Strong Interest Inventory (SII) Vocational Preference Inventory (VPI)
Derailers	Hogan Development Survey

Conclusion

Leadership is a multifaceted construct that cannot possibly be assessed using a single construct, or a single instrument. The methods referred to in this chapter and the five domains of leadership assessment give a broad overview of the field and are by no means exhaustive. The choice of psychometric instruments is practically limitless. While there are many excellent assessment measures available, it is important to be discerning and not just choose the cheapest or most simplified. A poorly developed and/or misused psychometric instrument can sometimes do more harm than not using one at all.

That being said, when psychometric tests are used in line with the needs of the organisation and the requirements of the job, in a way that maximises the benefit to the individual and organisation, the value will far surpass the cost. If one works with skilled assessment practitioners and reputable assessment measures, this will ensure that one's organisation gains every advantage from using assessments for leadership.

Endnotes

1   Deloitte, 2014.
2   Development Dimensions International, 2015.
3   Antonakis, Ciancolo & Sternberg, 2004.
4   Bass et al., 2003; Howell & Avolio, 1993; Rickards, Chen & Moger, 2001.
5   Liu et al., 2013; Long et al., 2012.
6   Obiwuru et al., 2011; Pillai, Schriesheim & Williams, 1999.
7   Goleman, 2000.
8   Development Dimensions International, 2015.
9   Charan, Drotter & Noel, 2001.
10   Conger & Fulmer, 2003.
11   Bell, 1999.
12   Berry, Carpenter & Barratt, 2012.
13   Berry et al., 2012; Ones, Viswesvaran & Reiss, 1996.
14   Hogan, Barrett & Hogan, 2007.
15   Slevin, 1972.
16   Dilchert & Ones, 2009.
17   Fleenor et al., 2010; Napper, 2013.
18   Connelly & Ones, 2010.
19   Kirkpatrick & Locke, 1991.
20   Kirkpatrick & Locke, 1991.
21   Bass, 1985.
22   Gardner, 1989.
23   Lowder, 2007.
24   Braddy et al., 2014.
25   Sjöberg, 2008.
26   Judge et al., 2002; Sjöberg, 2008.
27   Judge, Colbert & Ilies, 2004; Zhang, Sternberg & Rayner, 2012.
28   Guillén & Florent-Treacy, 2011.
29   Quinn, 1996.
30   Burke, 2006; Gaddis & Foster, 2015.
31   Hogan, Curphy & Hogan, 1994.
32   Judge et al., 2002.
33   McCrae & Costa, 1987.
34   Judge et al., 2002.
35   Lord, de Vader & Alliger, 1986.
36   Larsen & Ketelaar, 1989.
37   Hill & Ritchie, 1977.
38   Judge et al., 2002.
39   Hogan et al. 1994.
40   Hogan et al., 2007; Kirkpatrick & Locke, 1991.
41   McCrae & Sutin, 2009.
42   Judge et al., 2002.
43   Judge et al., 2002.
44   Barrick & Mount, 1991.
45   Judge et al., 2002.
46   Judge et al., 2004.
47   see Zhang, Sternberg, & Rayner (et al., 2012.
48   Zhang et al., 2012.
49   Kerr et al., 2005.
50   Bar-On, 1997; Goleman, Boyatzis & McKee, 2002; Dulewicz & Higgs, 1999; Mayer et al., 2003.
51   Kerr et al., 2005.
52   Rosete & Ciarrochi, 2005.
53   Cennamo & Gardner, 2008.
54   Thomas, Dickson & Bliese, 2001.
55   Kirkpatrick & Locke, 1991.
56   Gaddis & Foster, 2015; McCall & Lombardo, 1983.
57   Gaddis & Foster, 2015.

References

Antonakis, J, Ciancolo, AT & Sternberg, RJ. 2004. *The nature of leadership*. Thousand Oaks, CA: Sage Publications, Inc.

Bar-On, R. 1997. *Development of the Bar-On EQ-I: A measure of emotional intelligence*. Paper presented at the 105th Annual Convention of the American Psychological Association, Chicago.

Barrick, MR & Mount, MK. 1991. 'The big five personality dimensions and job performance: A meta-analysis'. *Personnel Psychology*, 44(1):1-26.

Bass, BM. 1985. *Leadership and performance beyond expectations*. New York, NY: Free Press.

Bass, BM, Avolio, BJ, Jung, DI & Berson, Y. 2003. 'Predicting unit performance by assessing transformational and transactional leadership'. *Journal of Applied Psychology*, 88(2):207-218.

Bell, A. 1999. 'How to use behavior-based structured interviewing'. *Workforce*, 1 October [Online]. Available: http://www.workforce.com/1999/10/01/how-to-use-behavior-based-structured-interviewing/. [Accessed 1 June 2016].

Berry, CM, Carpenter, NC & Barratt, CL. 2012. 'Do other-reports of counterproductive work behavior provide an incremental contribution over self-reports? A meta-analytic comparison.' *Journal of Applied Psychology*, 97(3):613-636.

Braddy, PW, Gooty, J, Fleenor, JW & Yammarino, F2014. 'Leader behaviors and career derailment potential: A multi-analytic method examination of rating source and self-other agreement'. *The Leadership Quarterly*, 25(2):373-390.

Burke, RJ. 2006. 'Why leaders fail: Exploring the darkside'. *International Journal of Manpower*, 27(1):91-100.

Cennamo, L & Gardner, D. 2008. 'Generational differences in work values, outcomes, and person-organisation values fit'. *Journal of Managerial Psychology*, 23(8):891–906.

Charan, R, Drotter, S & Noel, J. 2001. *The leadership pipeline: How to build the leadership-powered company.* San Francisco, CA: Jossey-Bass.

Conger, JA & Fulmer, RM. 2003. 'Developing your leadership pipeline'. *Harvard Business Review*, 1–10, December.

Connelly, BS & Ones, D. 2010. 'An other perspective on personality: Meta-analytic integration of observers' accuracy and predictive validity'. *Psychological Bulletin*, 136(6):1092–1122.

Deloitte. 2014. *Global human capital trends 2014: Engaging the 21st-century workforce.* London, UK: Deloitte University Press.

Development Dimensions International. 2015. *Ready-now leaders: 25 findings to meet tomorrow's business challenges (global leadership forecast 2014/2015).* Pittsburgh, PA: Development Dimensions International.

Dilchert, S & Ones, DS. 2009. 'Assessment center dimensions: Individual differences correlates and meta-analytic incremental validity'. *International Journal of Selection and Assessment*, 17(3):254–270.

Dulewicz, V & Higgs, M. 1999. 'Can emotional intelligence be measured and developed?' *Leadership & Organizational Development Journal*, 20(5):242–253.

Fleenor, JW, Smither, JW, Atwater, LE & Braddy, PW. 2010. 'Self–other rating agreement in leadership: A review'. *The Leadership Quarterly*, 21(6):1005–1034.

Gaddis, BH & Foster, JL. 2015. 'A meta-analysis of dark side personality characteristics and critical work behaviors among leaders across the globe: Findings and implications for leadership development and executive coaching'. *Applied Psychology*, 64(1):25–54.

Gardner, JW. 1989. *On leadership.* New York, NY: Free Press.

Goleman, D. 2000. Leadership that gets results. *Harvard Business Review,* March-April. [Online]. Available: https://hbr.org/2000/03/leadership-that-gets-results. [Accessed 1 June 2016].

Goleman, D, Boyatzis, R & McKee, A. 2002. *Primal leadership: Learning to lead with emotional intelligence.* Boston, MA: Harvard Business School Press.

Guillén, L & Florent-Treacy, E. 2011. *Emotional intelligence and leadership effectiveness: The mediating influence of collaborative behaviors.* INSEAD Working Paper. [Online]. Available: http://dmcodyssey.org/wp-content/uploads/2013/08/THE-EMOTIONAL-COMPETENCE-FRAMEWORK_1.pdf. [Accessed 1 June 2016].

Hill, NC & Ritchie, JB. 1977. 'The effect of self-esteem on leadership and achievement: A paradigm and a review'. *Group & Organization Management*, 2(4):491–503.

Hogan, J, Barrett, P & Hogan, R. 2007. 'Personality measurement, faking, and employment selection'. *Journal of Applied Psychology*, 92(5):1270–1285.

Hogan, R, Curphy, GJ & Hogan, J. 1994. 'What we know about leadership: Effectiveness and personality'. *American Psychologist*, 49(6):493–504.

Howell, JM & Avolio, BJ. 1993. 'Transformational leadership, transactional leadership, locus of control, and support for innovation: Key predictors of consolidated-business-unit performance'. *Journal of Applied Psychology*, 78(6):891–902.

Judge, TA, Bono, JE, Ilies, R & Gerhardt, MW. 2002. 'Personality and leadership: A qualitative and quantitative review'. *Journal of Applied Psychology*, 87(4):765-780.

Judge, TA, Colbert, AE & Ilies, R. 2004. Intelligence and leadership: A quantitative review and test of theoretical propositions. *Journal of Applied Psychology*, 89(3):542–552.

Kerr, R, Gavin, J, Heaton, N & Boyle, E. 2005. 'Emotional intelligence and leadership effectiveness'. *Leadership & Organization Development Journal*, 27(4):265–279.

Kirkpatrick, SA & Locke, EA. 1991. 'Leadership: Do traits matter?' *The Executive*, 5(2):48–60.

Larsen, RJ & Ketelaar, T. 1989. 'Extraversion, neuroticism, and susceptibility to positive and negative mood induction procedures'. *Personality and Individual Differences*, 10(12):1221–1228.

Liu, Z, Cai, Z, Li, J, Shi, S & Fang, Y. 2013. 'Leadership style and employee turnover intentions: A social identity perspective'. *Career Development International*, 18(3):305–324.

Long, CS, Thean, LY, Wan Ismail, WK & Jusoh, A. 2012. 'Leadership styles and employees' turnover intention: Exploratory study of academic staff in a Malaysian College'. *World Applied Sciences Journal* 19(4):575–581.

Lord, RG, de Vader, CL & Alliger, GM. 1986. 'A meta-analysis of the relation between personality traits and leadership perceptions: An application of validity generalization procedures'. *Journal of Applied Psychology*, 71(3):402–410.

Lowder, BT. 2007. 'Five dimensions of effective leadership: An analysis of leadership attributes & behaviors'. *Social Science Research Network*. [Online]. Available: http://dx.doi.org/10.2139/ssrn.975559.

Mayer, JD, Salovey, P, Caruso, DR & Sitarenios, G. 2003. Measuring emotional intelligence with the MSCEIT V2.0. *Emotion* 3(1):97–105.

McCall, MW, Jr. & Lombardo, MM. 1983. *Off the track: Why and how successful executives get derailed* (Technical Report No. 21). Greensboro, NC: Center for Creative Leadership.

McCrae, RR & Costa, PT. 1987. 'Validation of the five-factor model of personality across instruments and observers'. *Journal of Personality and Social Psychology*, 52(1):81–90.

McCrae, RR & Sutin, AR. 2009. 'Openness to experience'. In MR Leary & RH Hoyle (eds). *Handbook of individual differences in social behavior*. New York, NY: Guilford. 257–273.

Napper, CN. 2013. 'Exploring the structural relationships between personality and 360-degree feedback'. Unpublished doctoral dissertation, College of Education, Louisiana, LA: Louisiana Technical University.

Obiwuru, TC, Okwu, AT, Akpa, VO & Nwankere, IA. 2011. 'Effects of leadership style on organizational performance: A survey of selected small scale enterprises in Ikosi-Ketu council development area of Lagos state, Nigeria'. *Australian Journal of Business Management Research*, 1(7):100–111.

Ones, DS, Viswesvaran, C & Reiss, AD. 1996. 'Role of social desirability in personality testing for personnel selection: The red herring'. *Journal of Applied Psychology*, 81(6):660–679.

Pillai, R, Schriesheim, CA & Williams, ES. 1999. 'Fairness perceptions and trust as mediators for transformational and transactional leadership: A two-sample study'. *Journal of Management*, 25(6):897–933.

Quinn, RE. 1996. *Deep change*. San Francisco, CA: Jossey-Bass.

Rickards, T, Chen, M-W & Moger, S. 2001. 'Development of a self-report instrument for exploring team factor, leadership and performance relationships'. *British Journal of Management*, 12(3):243–250.

Rosete, D & Ciarrochi, J. 2005. 'Emotional intelligence and its relationship to workplace performance outcomes of leadership effectiveness'. *Leadership & Organization Development Journal*, 26(5):388–399.

Sjöberg, S. 2008. 'What do we know about traits predicting leader emergence and leader effectiveness?'. *Frontiers in Leadership Research*, 8:1–11.

Slevin, D. 1972. 'The assessment center: Breakthrough in management appraisal and development'. *Personnel Journal*, 51(4):255–261.

Thomas, JL, Dickson, MW & Bliese, PD. 2001. 'Values predicting leader performance in the U.S. Army Reserve Officer Training Corps Assessment Center: Evidence for a personality-mediated model'. *The Leadership Quarterly*, 2(2):181–196.

Zhang, L-F, Sternberg, RJ & Rayner, S. 2012. *Handbook of intellectual styles: Preferences in cognition, learning, and thinking*. New York, NY: Springer.

Additional readings

Ones, DS & Dilchert, S. 2009. 'How special are executives? How special should executive selection be? Observations and recommendations'. *Industrial and Organizational Psychology*, 2(2):163–170.

Paunonen, SV & LeBel, EP. 2012. 'Socially desirable responding and its elusive effects on the validity of personality assessments'. *Journal of Personality and Social Psychology*, 103(1):158–175.

Chapter 4

LEADERSHIP DEVELOPMENT: PRINCIPLES, APPROACHES AND PROCESSES

Nancy Keeshan and Sharmla Chetty

Duke Corporate Education (Duke CE) conducted a global CEO study in 2013 in order to gather reactions about the rapidly changing organisational, and in particular the business, context. It became clear that leaders around the world were struggling in the new context. Optimising internal strengths and executing a good strategy was no longer enough. To succeed, organisations would have to be more agile, adaptive and able to accelerate. In this context leaders are the greatest levers to see and seize these new opportunities and create organisations that can thrive.

Leaders need to be ready to step up to a new role: one that embraces different ways of perceiving the world, making sense of it, and catalysing action. In today's volatile, unpredictable world our traditional pillars of organisational stability – strategy, organisational models, and capabilities – are being continually challenged. We believe that there is great opportunity inherent in this volatility, but organisations are at risk of losing their way if they hang on to old models of success.

Over the next few years after 2013, Duke CE collaborated with thought leaders from neuroscience, business anthropology, and communication to discover how leadership development needed to change to prepare leaders for thriving in a volatile, uncertain, complex and ambiguous world.[1] This chapter describes the outcome of that collaboration: an iterative process around a set of capabilities to prepare leaders for what is next: our Perceive-Sense-making-Choreograph Framework. The chapter proceeds by first giving an overview of this framework, followed by describing each of the three capabilities making up the framework: Perception; Sense-making. and Choreography.

Developing New Capabilities to "Rewire" Leaders to See, Think and Act Differently: Our Perceive-Sense-making-Choreograph Framework

If you identify yourself as an organisational leader, Chief Learning Officer (CLO), or Human Resources Leader, you will understand this new reality very well. it is likely that every day, you encounter some degree of volatility, uncertainty, complexity and ambiguity. Globalisation and technological advancements have disrupted business models in profound ways – this trend will only continue. Basic assumptions, heuristics and mental models that worked in the past are failing us fast. Experiences that previously led to solutions will not stand the test of time as the pace of change continues to accelerate. What are leaders to do, and how can they navigate the complexity of our context?

The answer is not found in relying on previous experiences and seeking the assumed right answers. In some instances, relying on the past may actually be counter-productive in this ever-changing context. From Duke CE's experience in leadership development, we offer an alternative. Leaders need to have the capacity to understand context and how things work systemically. Sounds simple, but to do this really effectively requires "rewiring" the way the mind thinks and tackles problems.

In our collaboration with ReD Associates, a business anthropology firm based in New York and Copenhagen, we found great value in their approach to unlocking organisational challenges by combining the human sciences with management science. This powerful combination of perspectives requires the development of new capabilities to "rewire" leaders to see, think and act differently.

This rewiring centres around three meta-capabilities, as depicted in Figure 4.1.

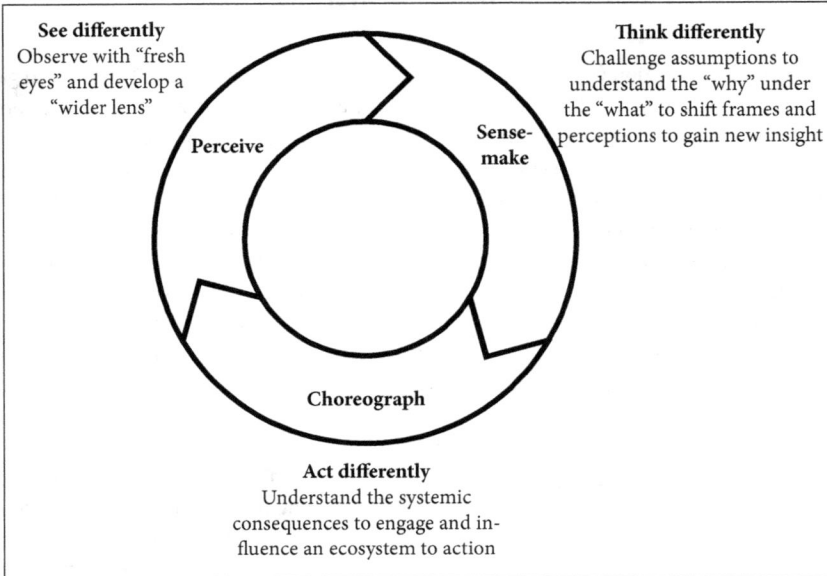

See differently
Observe with "fresh eyes" and develop a "wider lens"

Perceive

Sense-make

Think differently
Challenge assumptions to understand the "why" under the "what" to shift frames and perceptions to gain new insight

Choreograph

Act differently
Understand the systemic consequences to engage and influence an ecosystem to action

Figure 4.1: Our Perceive-Sense-making-Choreograph (PSC) Framework

The PSC Framework is based on three interdependent actions:

- **Perceiving:** Leaders learn to recognise the limitations of old mental models; re-frame organisational challenges or opportunities within a particular context; and engage with the relevant human factors surrounding the issue.
- **Sense-making:** Leaders deeply understand the specific context and the people in it; find patterns in insights collected from multiple perspectives; and continuously iterate on potential solutions to determine the best approach for the particular context.
- **Choreographing:** Leaders identify key points of leverage within an ecosystem surrounding the context; manage important interests, stage and sequence activities; and direct collaborative action to achieve success.

These capabilities re-orientate leaders for sustainable success, regardless of the rate of change. They serve as a continuously iterative process for understanding any unfamiliar situation. In the balance of our chapter, we will outline these capabilities in more detail and provide insights on how one can prepare for uncertainty, at both the individual and organisational levels. We explain the challenge and solution and illustrate this through the work we have done with different clients as well as other organisational examples. We conclude each section with questions that the reader can consider for his/her particular context.

As Peter Senge points out in a 2015 issue of the *Stanford Social Innovation Review*, in order to win in the new organisational context, leaders must see the larger system; foster reflection;

generate conversation; and shift from reactive problem solving to co-creating the future. We aim to demonstrate how these capabilities can lead to just that.[2]

Perceiving: See Differently

The Perception challenge

How leaders perceive the context around them is developed over multiple years, resulting in the equivalent of a default setting in the brain. Over time brains become more efficient by creating shortcuts based on familiar patterns that allow a person to glance at a situation or data; compare it to a previous experience; and instantly generate an answer. This sort of automatic thinking is highly efficient in a relatively static context. However, this automation can be problematic in a dynamic and uncertain context.

In *The Moment of Clarity*, Christian Madsbjerg and Mikkel Rasmussen of ReD Associates indicate that this automatic thinking tends to result from an "inside-out" orientation, where organisations view situations from their own vantage point.[3] Figure 4.2 illustrates this orientation.

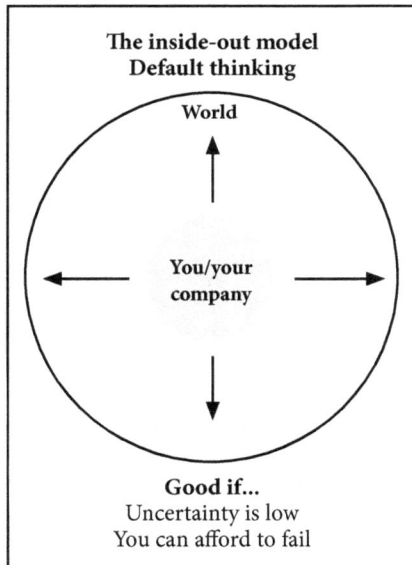

The inside-out model
Default thinking

World

You/your
company

Good if...
Uncertainty is low
You can afford to fail

Figure 4.2: Inside-out model
Source: *ReD Associates*[4]

Madsbjerg and Rasmussen describe the dangers of default thinking: They offer the story of LEGO, a very successful toy manufacturer, which began to suffer losses in early 2000. LEGO had gradually shifted its focus from the "brick" to the brand. They began making assumptions about what kids want based on focus-group data and market trends without directly observing what kids do when they play.[5]

All too often, leaders rely on data or assumptions when they make decisions. Data cannot tell one why people act as they do. They tell one only end results. Assumptions can be biased and also become orthodoxies within companies and across industries. Unless frequently questioned and tested, this comfortable sense of familiarity can blind leaders to reality. Once LEGO began directly observing and interviewing kids about why and how they play, they realised that their initial assumptions were wrong. As they moved "back to the brick," the organisation flourished. This is why effective perceiving skills is important. We revisit this case study later in the chapter.

Overcoming the Perception challenge

Leaders need to see the world with fresh eyes, in a way similar to the way in which a child perceives. Children encountering an activity for the first time approach new experiences without preconceived notions of how things are or should be. They experiment with various approaches. They learn through iterative attempts. They incessantly ask, "Why?" This is essentially the "beginner's mindset". Leaders need to regain these child-like qualities. They need to leave assumptions and biases behind in order to look as objectively as possible at what *actually* happens in a context. Adopting this "outside-in" perspective can help companies think differently about the context around them. Figure 4.3 depicts this perspective.

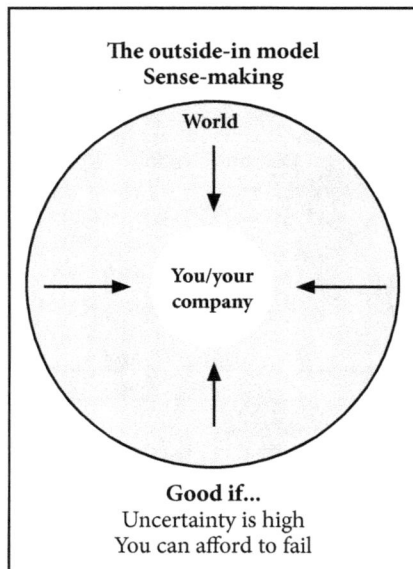

The outside-in model
Sense-making

World

↓

You/your
company

→   ←

↑

Good if...
Uncertainty is high
You can afford to fail

Figure 4.3: Outside-In model
Source: ReD Associates[6]

At first, it is difficult to overcome our inherent "confirmation bias". The tendency is to jump to solutions based on superficial understanding. With continued practice and reflection, a leader will begin to perceive events and actions that may disprove engrained mental models. By asking questions of people in the context, leaders will find out what, how and why things happen; for example, who has power; who needs to be involved in decisions or actions, and how; why steps in a process must happen in a certain order. Freeing oneself to examine or inquire about a context without judgement is critical to being able to understand in depth how things work in an unfamiliar setting.

Perception applications

A pension company noticed that they were losing clients at around age 55, just as they were nearing retirement. Traditionally, the company had believed that once you start with an employer, you would stay for 40 years, and then access your pension. Communication was kept to a minimum. The expectation was that people would sign up for the company pension scheme, and then leave it alone. In reality, people were no longer taking a job for life. Employees that joined company pension schemes were no longer secure members until retirement. This is a case where the company's orthodoxy caused a misperception of customer needs.

This organisation applied the tools of anthropology (= study of humans) and ethnography (= customs of individual peoples and cultures) to better understand why customers were leaving. In-depth interviews revealed that customers across various age ranges wanted to be more actively involved in their pension planning and preferred more advice and counselling early on (and especially as they got ready to access the pension). The company's overall performance improved dramatically once they adjusted to their customers' wishes.[7]

Another application is to consider a different market segment: the millennials. As millennials enter the job market, it is important for financial services companies to understand fully their attitudes toward money and risk. Assuming that millennials think about money, savings and insurance in the same way as baby boomers do is fraught with risk.

Again, using the tools of ethnography, a financial services institution decided to test their perception and sent employees to visit and interview diverse millennials in their homes. Without exception, all the employees came back with new insights about what this demographic wanted as well as some innovative ideas for delivering value to this group.

A third and final application revolves around a South African bank. When leaders within the bank struggled to understand a non-traditional consumer base at the bottom of the pyramid, Duke CE took them on a week-long immersion in India. While there, the bank's leaders were equipped with a perceiving toolkit, enabling them to suspend judgement and evaluate what is truly there, rather than relying on one's own unconscious bias. Delegates from the bank spent time interacting with merchants around Mumbai; followed service-delivery workers who belonged to a traditionally unbanked segment; and spent an afternoon in a dense slum, observing the informal economy there. These exposures changed a monolithic and de-personalised "segment" into individual stories and led to key insights.

In the above applications, leaders' mindsets changed by teaching tools of perception and allowing learners to see customers in a new light by using their senses (seeing, hearing and feeling) to understand the market deeply.

Perception implications for oneself and one's organisation: Questions to consider

Table 4.1 provides some of the more important questions to consider with regard to Perceiving.

Table 4.1: Questions relating to Perceiving

1.	What assumptions are inherent in decisions you make about your organisation and business?
2.	How might your assumptions be flawed?
3.	How might these flaws be impacting your strategy, operations and overall organisation?
4.	How might you as a leader learn to look at the world with fresh eyes?
5.	What types of things can you and your organisation do to improve your perceiving skills and test out your assumptions?

Sense-making: Think Differently

The Sense-making challenge

After gleaning new insights from better perception of the context, leaders should have multiple perspectives on an issue. How do you bring these different perspectives together in a coherent way? Any context is surrounded and supported by an underlying system, or hidden scaffolding, that governs norms, rules, incentives and behaviour. To make sense of the context, it is important to identify how the system works; why the people act as they do within that system or context; and what action is needed to influence that system. This is where effective sense-making comes in.

Overcoming the Sense-making challenge

The ultimate goal of sense-making is to create meaning. Sense-making begins with a search for patterns that emerge from observations and conversations initiated in the perceiving stage. Once data is gathered from perceiving with a beginner's mindset, leaders should ask:

- What stands out as unusual or different from original expectations?
- What unique trends were found in how people acted? Is there a discrepancy between what people *say* and what they actually *do*?
- How does the larger context shape people's actions? Inevitably, leaders discover that a particular context is surrounded by a larger ecosystem that contributes to overall understanding.
- What are the interrelationships and/or interdependencies between people and institutions?
- Do I need to move away from traditional ways of thinking?

Leaders must avoid reverting to default thinking, and jumping to solutions; or letting personal biases or old mental models affect their sense-making. Multiple hypotheses that might explain the observed phenomenon should be considered before settling on a few to test with stakeholders and the greater ecosystem in the context.

Ultimately, effective sense-making helps leaders create a temporarily static view of a context in a systemic way. Once the ecosystem surrounding the issue is fully mapped, leaders can more clearly see leverage points and develop strategies to influence the system.

Sense-making applications

Let us take, for example, an organisation which wanted to improve sense-making and decision-making skills in their leaders. To overcome biases and build skills, the organisation decided to teach the sense-making process in a "safe" practice field, without direct relevance to their daily business. The organisation believed, and we concurred, that practising the skill of sense-making was crucial to shifting mindsets, and also that it would be difficult to shift mindsets if we remained inside the organisation, surrounded by its orthodoxies and assumptions.

They used our PSC Framework to understand better how a new infrastructure project would affect the people in a specific market. Teams of individuals were sent out to explore different aspects of the city: transportation, infrastructure, and the diverse needs of different neighbourhoods. Teams came back to the classroom and compared their various perspectives and insights together. As they explored, they also gained new insights through their improved perception. Specific patterns began to emerge, and the teams were able to depict visually how the entire system fitted together. As they mapped this ecosystem, they began to understand the number and diversity of stakeholders that would need to be considered if any change was to be implemented.

The company then took the sense-making approach inside the organisation, so as to understand better employee attitudes toward the amount of change happening in the company. Their insights allowed the leaders to handle employee frustration and resistance more effectively. Through this sense-making process, leaders' perceptions became sharper as they continued to gain deeper understanding of the human needs surrounding an issue. The sense-making sessions helped shift leaders' mindsets and provided a repeatable process for using sense-making in other organisational initiatives.

Sense-making implications for oneself and one's organisation: Questions to consider

Table 4.2 provides some of the more important questions to consider with regard to Sense-making.

Table 4.2: Questions relating to Sense-making

1.	How do you consider viewpoints from stakeholders in order to understand internal and external organisational challenges fully?
2.	What are the tools and resources that enable you to identify patterns and develop insights from multiple perspectives in order to make sense of the context?
3.	How do you ensure that this "outside-in" perspective is an ongoing practice?

Choreographing: Act Differently

The Choreographing challenge

Leaders in today's complex world will rarely be able to act alone to bring about change. They need to create a collective of stakeholders and partners to ensure enduring impact. Often, leaders are required to influence those over whom they have no control. This is more easily said than done and is the essence of choreographing: bringing disparate parties and stakeholders together to move forward and seamlessly accomplish a goal or implement a strategy.

Overcoming the Choreograph challenge

To choreograph, leaders first need the deep understanding that emerges from the sense-making phase to create a strategy for successful action. Deep understanding of a context and its surrounding ecosystem helps identify structural as well as attitudinal barriers to overcome. It also highlights shared as well as competing needs, priorities and interests among stakeholders. As the leader surveys the context, he/she can more clearly see points of leverage available to address the situation. A strategy to influence and change the system can be developed. The leader can stage and sequence actions to execute his/her strategy.

Given the complexity of ecosystems, the strategy will most likely involve influencing diverse groups of people into taking collective action towards a specific goal. Leaders may need to negotiate trade-offs between groups of stakeholders, or help stakeholders to understand that actions must occur in a certain sequence. Here is where the "art" of leadership and diplomacy – building relationships, establishing trust, negotiating needs and interests – comes into play. The development of leadership skills for the choreography stage is directly linked to the understanding and empathy that is derived from the perceiving and sense-making phases.

Choreographing applications

Perhaps it is easiest to explain choreography by providing an example of what should NOT happen. Ron Adner, in his book *The Wide Lens*,[8] tells the story of Michelin's introduction of run-flat tyres. This was a great innovation that foundered as a result of the lack of choreography. Michelin was unable to recruit enough service stations to invest in the technology and equipment needed to service the nitrogen-filled tyres. By not considering the entire ecosystem and who needed to support its product, Michelin's success was limited. The value proposition was impressive: being able to drive up to 100 miles with a flat tyre. However, the ecosystem to support the innovation was virtually non-existent.

Pharmaceutical companies have discovered that medical compliance needs to be carefully choreographed and is often context-specific, which can be gleaned through perceiving and sense-making. Think about the complex nature of doctor-patient relationships and how these vary from country to country. Drug delivery systems are also very different. It is clear that one size does not fit all. Pharmaceutical companies need to develop very different approaches based on each context. By perceiving how things work and understanding the systemic interdependencies, they have been able to overcome obstacles and gain higher levels of patient compliance. In essence, choreography goes beyond mere execution. It is comprised of deep understanding of the system and all its components are combined with a context-specific strategy in order to ensure results with the end-users.

Another company in the pharmaceutical industry conducted perceiving and sense-making sessions around one specific drug. Programme participants observed doctors' consulting rooms and talked with hospital administrators, wholesalers, and end-users of their drug. Again, new insights emerged about how the whole ecosystem worked, providing new ideas about ways to package, market and sell the drug.

Choreographing implications for oneself and one's organisation: Questions to consider

Table 4.3 provides some of the more important questions to consider with regard to Choreographing.

Table 4.3: Questions relating to Choreographing

1.	How do you identify the points of leverage within your ecosystem that will enable you to organise more effectively?
2.	How do you manage and build relationships with stakeholder groups that are outside the traditional boundaries of your organisation but could serve as viable and useful partners to achieve specific organisational objectives?
3.	How does your organisation integrate context into its strategy?

Figure 4.4 provides a detailed view of the iterative process making up the Duke CE PSC Framework.

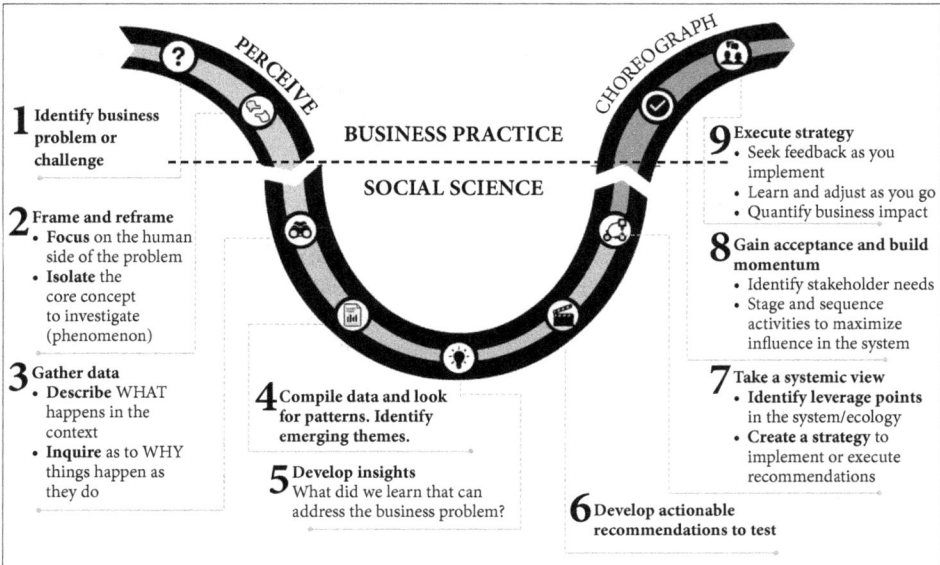

Figure 4.4: Duke CE PSC Framework: A detailed view of the iterative process
Source: *Adapted from ReD Associates*[9]

Making the Perceive-Sense-making-Choreography Framework Practical: The Case of LEGO

As one looks at an organisation with regard to approaching a situation using perceiving, sense-making and choreography, it is helpful to think through the process in a step-by-step approach. In order to demonstrate a practical application of the PSC iterative process, let us use a fairly well-known case study, LEGO.

In 2005, LEGO looked around the landscape of children's play and believed that electronic games were changing how children played. Their assumption was that video games, particularly PlayStation, were easy, fun, and offered instant traction. This assumption led LEGO away from their primary building bricks and into less demanding toys. However, when this strategic gamble didn't pay off, LEGO was left trying to salvage their business. They decided to revisit their initial assumptions by using a sense-making process. Below, we apply the PSC framework to LEGO's journey.

Perceiving by LEGO

- *Step P1: Define the organisation issue*

    LEGO/initially approached their business through the lens of management science. Worried about declining sales, they asked: "How can we sell more toys?"

- *Step P2: Frame and reframe*

    Start with the business problem, describe the unfamiliar aspects, and then consider the human and social phenomena surrounding the problem. Select and test a phenomenon. Repeat, clarify, and modify as necessary. To reframe this strategic business question as a human phenomenon means to ask, "Why do kids play?" Asking the question in this way opened LEGO up to possibility, rather than incorrect assumptions.

- *Step P3: Gather data*

    Now move into the field, practising ethnography in order to understand the phenomenon more deeply. Look at observable practices and attitudes to try to understand the underlying drivers. What do people say when interviewed? What do they actually do, regardless of what they say? What kind of values, attitudes, and practices are present? LEGO quite literally observed kids playing; spoke to them and their parents and grandparents about what they saw; and gathered data in a variety of media. For example, asking children to show off their most prized possession revealed things such as a boy's sneaker, worn down in certain places because of repeated practising of skateboarding tricks. This one prized possession later became key to generating powerful insights about why children play.

Sense-making by LEGO

- *Step S1: Look for patterns and themes*

    After gathering data, sort, structure and analyse them until patterns appear. Move away from individual data points to a broad finding that has explanatory power. These patterns are compared to initial assumptions in order to create rich discussions. LEGO learned that playing was full of skill, complexity, and mastery. *This was the exact opposite of their initial assumptions.* It was discovered only through ethnographic data collection. Children wanted to be challenged; show off their skills and accomplishments; and move away from their comfort zone.

- *Step S2: Develop insights*

  Distil patterns and themes to key insights about the phenomenon. A good insight will shed new light on consumers or the market; clearly point to an opportunity; and explain an observed reality. They are often simple, memorable, intuitive, and even provocative. LEGO developed insights that included: "Our toys should challenge kids," "Our toys should enable kids to show off skills," "Our toys should be as complex as kids' worlds." You can see how these insights move from observation of how children play into connecting to the organisational world of LEGO.

- *Step S3: Develop actionable recommendations to test*

  Each insight will suggest a course of action. Using an iterative process of successive approximation, start testing each recommendation with stakeholders and customers. Find the recommendation that creates the most organisational impact. In LEGO's case, this was ultimately moving away from electronic toys and refocusing attention on the basic brick, and creating more and more challenging options for customers.

Choreography[i]

- *Step C1: Create a strategy by taking a systemic view*

  Think broadly about the system surrounding the phenomenon, and find leverage points. Understand the needs and interests of decision-makers as well as end-users. Also consider key stakeholders inside the company. LEGO included parents and grandparents in their perceiving and sense-making process, and created solutions that appealed to these buyers. Internal stakeholders also had to be persuaded to go "back to the brick."

- *Step C2: Gain acceptance and build momentum*

  Often it is important to build internal organisational awareness and support before tackling the external market. Business people tend to have an inherent bias for quantitative, data. They may be sceptical about insights generated from qualitative research. Help internal divisions to see the value of the insights. In some cases, comparing insights generated from the sense-making process to existing organisational data will reveal patterns in quantitative data that were previously unseen.

---

i   Note: We do not actually have access to the specific steps that LEGO used to implement their strategy, so we are basing our suggestions on actions that other clients have taken in similar settings.

> • **Step C3: Execute the strategy**
>
> Implement the strategy and continuously test and adapt to feedback in the system to produce value to the business. After focusing on the basic brick to stabilise the company, LEGO eventually expanded their focus to electronic toys and even animated movies. LEGO bounced back, and attributed their financial recovery partially to their ability to understand children's play more deeply.

Conclusion

The PSC framework points to a new angle for leadership development. With practice, these three meta-capabilities and the iterative process of employing them can create leaders who are able and willing to take on unfamiliar challenges and contexts. The deep understanding that is achieved through repeated application of the three-stage process of perceiving, sense-making and choreography can produce unexpectedly simple, yet wildly innovative, solutions to stubborn issues.

Duke CE believes that the best way to practise these capabilities is to immerse learners in multiple unfamiliar contexts while providing just-in-time support along with personalised feedback on a leader's performance in context. This experiential learning should ideally start in a relatively "safe" practice area, but can gradually be focused on solving real-world issues that can add immediate value to organisations. Carefully structured learning contexts and experiences can "rewire" leaders by supporting them as they act their way into new ways of thinking. Through immersive, problem-based learning, leaders can literally carve new neural pathways in their brains, and become more agile in addressing complex problems in a volatile world.

Endnotes

1. Duke Corporate Education, 2013.
2. Senge, Hamilton & Kania, 2015.
3. Madsbjerg & Rasmussen, 2014.
4. Madsbjerg & Rasmussen, 2014.
5. Madsbjerg & Rasmussen, 2014.
6. Madsbjerg & Rasmussen, 2014.
7. Giroux, Gugelmann & Okada, 2016.
8. Adner, 2012.
9. Duke CE model adapted from ReD Associates.

References

Adner, R. 2012. *The wide lens: A new strategy for innovation*. London, UK: Penguin.

Duke Corporate Education (Duke CE). 2013. *Leading in context: 2013 CEO study*. [Online]. Available: http://www. dukece.com/wp-content/uploads/2015/06/LeadingInContext_web_newlogo.pdf. [Accessed 15 June 2016].

Giroux, J, Gugelmann, F & Okada, J. 2016. 'Dialogue classic – Lego and Cisco Know what business anthropology is. Do you?' *Dialogue*, 4 January. [Online]. Available: http://dialoguereview.com/sensemaking-brick-brick/. [Accessed 15 June 2016].

Madsbjerg, C & Rasmussen, M. 2014. *The moment of clarity: Using the human sciences to solve your toughest business problems*. Boston, MA: Harvard Business Review Press.

Merchant, N. 2012. *11 Rules for creating value in the social era*. Boston, MA: Harvard Business Review Press.

Senge, P, Hamilton, H & Kania, J. 2015. 'The dawn of system leadership'. *Stanford Social Innovation Review*. [Online]. Available: http://ssir.org/articles/entry/the_dawn_of_system_leadership. [Accessed 15 June 2016].

Chapter 5

LEADERSHIP COACHING
Aletta Odendaal

Given the complexity of challenges and uncertainties experienced by organisations globally combined with an increasingly multicultural and diverse operating context, it is not surprising that CEOs across the globe have identified human capital challenges as fundamental for future growth and sustainability.[1] The development of effective leaders on all levels of the organisation is therefore more critical than ever before. In the past decade, leadership and executive coaching has emerged as a significant strategy and the most widely used intervention for leadership development.[2] Evidence is starting to emerge linking coaching in organisations to enhanced individual performance; subsequent skill development; enhanced wellbeing and coping; as well as improved attitudes and self-regulation.[3]

However, the fact that leadership coaching is a qualitatively different approach compared to other leadership development initiatives must be taken into account when implementing it within an organisation. Reviewing current industry standards, the typical leadership development mix suggested is 10% classroom (or formal) training, 20% coaching, and 70% experiential or ("stretched") activities and assignments.[4] Recent surveys further show that 72% of participating organisations used coaching as a leadership development activity. Eighty percent of organisations that conduct leadership development activities listed coaching as the most effective intervention.[i]

Notwithstanding the high demand for leadership coaching as a strategy for leadership development, there is still a shortage of evidence linking the process of leadership coaching to coaching outcomes as well as leadership research with coaching research.[5] Given the growing investment that individuals and organisations are placing in leadership coaching and the strong impact that coaching can have on organisational performance, coaching practitioners have to understand the knowledge base that guides their practice and be able to define what they do with and for their clients.[6]

Grounded in the ethos of coaching, I will provide a discussion of leadership coaching around a number of questions. The first question considered is around clarity of concepts: What is coaching, leadership coaching, and executive coaching? I will then consider critical success factors as well as an understanding of the purpose, perspectives and process to apply in order to enhance the likelihood of successful leadership coaching outcomes. A discussion of the areas of knowledge relevant to leadership coaching follows: What knowledge bases are relevant to leadership coaching? Which theories and models shape our practice and how do these fit the range of coaching contexts? I will conclude the chapter by discussing developments in the evaluation of coaching. Throughout the chapter I have indicated notable trends and leading business practices regarding leadership coaching.

Defining Coaching, Leadership and Executive Coaching

Typical attempts at defining coaching usually refer to the *purpose* or outcomes to be achieved: why is coaching needed?; the *type of clients or domain* where coaching is taking place: who makes use of coaching?; different *perspectives* applied in coaching: what are the theoretical approaches or methods used?; the *process* utilised: how is coaching applied?; or any combinations of the

---

i   Surveys conducted by the Conference Board of Canada, Hughes & Campbell (2009) and Chartered Institute of Personnel Development (CIPD) in 2015.

above.[7] However, it is not simply a matter of supporting a specific definition of coaching but rather of being aware that each type of coaching requires a specific set of skills, knowledge and competencies beyond generic coaching skills.

Coaching

In a review of coaching definitions it is evident that there is indeed a range of definitions, which are generally anchored in relationships, problem identification and goal-setting, transformational processes, and outcomes to be achieved. To this end Grant defines coaching as:

> *"A collaborative relationship formed between coach and coachee for the purpose of attaining professional or personal development outcomes which are valued by the coachee".*[8]

Of specific importance in this definition is the emphasis on both personal and professional business-related issues in coaching. Recurring themes that emerged from viewing different definitions are the emphasis on:

- Unlocking of potential to maximise and enhance performance;
- The conversation being collaborative and goal-directed;
- Ultimately aiming at personal, professional and organisational effectiveness; and
- Utilising appropriate strategies, tools and techniques for the benefit of the client and all stakeholders involved.[9]

Coaching in general is therefore strongly informed by a common set of principles: collaboration, accountability, awareness raising, responsibility, commitment, action planning and ultimately action.[10]

Leadership and executive coaching

Leadership coaching can be viewed as the coaching of a leader, executive and manager, the team and the wider organisation, with *leadership effectiveness* as the main outcome to be achieved.[11] The terms "leadership coaching" and "executive coaching" are often used interchangeably, notwithstanding some differences in content to be addressed and outcomes to be achieved. Leadership coaching is furthermore distinguished from mentoring, where the latter is seen more as an informal relationship with an experienced colleague.[12] The distinguishing features of leadership coaching are listed in Table 5.1.

Table 5.1: Distinguishing features of Leadership Coaching[13]

• A formal one-on-one relationship that extends to the team and organisational levels, typically provided by an external coach: a flexible and individualised process to achieve desired outcomes as determined by the individual and organisation
• A strong emphasis on how an individual leader exercises interpersonal influence towards the attainment of organisational goals. That is, the knowledge, skills and competencies associated with the formal role in the organisation, and attending to the particular needs of the leader in his/her role in the organisation
• Often informed by the use of psychometric and competency assessment and feedback tools enabling personal reflection on preferences, challenges, and ethical dilemmas

> - An emphasis on the transition from management to leadership; from an operational and task perspective to a strategic focus; and from controlling events to enabling others
> - The recognition of the importance of deeper-level transformations associated with leader identity formation, where the leader moves from an individual to a more relational and collective orientation as well as a value-based identity: authentic leadership

In addition to emphasising the coaching relationship, the processes, the context and the outcomes to be achieved, the above distinguishing features also differentiate leadership coaching from other leadership development interventions such as training and experiential (or stretched) assignments/projects. Additionally, there is a noticeable shift from human capital development in organisations towards the development of social capital,[14] where the interaction of the individual leader within the wider system becomes the key focus.

Accelerating Leadership Development through Coaching

Given the current challenges and trend in an increasingly complex working context, research and practice clearly indicate that leadership behaviour associated with historical results may not be the behaviour required to achieve future success. It is readily apparent that organisations are skilled at developing individual leader competencies but have not been equally skilled at transforming the leader's mindset from one level to the next.

A clear trend in leadership development is the transition from *horizontal* development approaches: knowledge, skills and competencies, to *vertical* leadership development: construct meaning from experiences and transform the consciousness.[15] Leadership and executive coaching has emerged as a popular strategy employed by organisations for vertical leadership development. Vertical development changes the way that leaders give meaning to their world, as well as how they think and need to process information differently. Figure 5.1 depicts this transition from horizontal to vertical development.

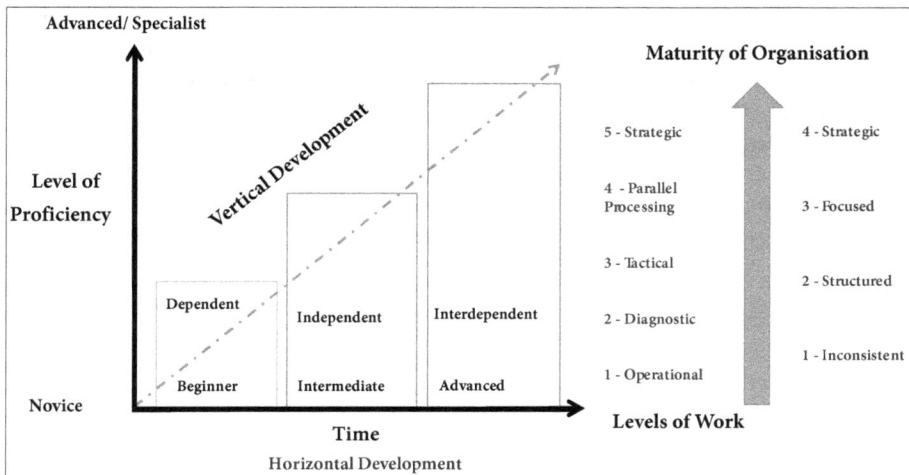

Figure 5.1: Vertical and horizontal leadership development
Sources: *Integrated from Bersin & Associates, 2009, 2013; Jaques, 2006; Kegan & Lahey, 2009; Petrie, 2013 (CCL)*[16]

As illustrated in Figure 5.1, people progress through different *stages of development*. The three most common stages of development are from dependence through independence to interdependence.[17] The leadership coach must therefore be cognisant of the fact that people in each stage will construct the meaning of situations, persons, events, and interactions differently. A plateau can also be reached. Therefore adults have to work consistently to keep growing, the focus being on continuous vertical development. While leaders think strategically about change, it is important to emphasise that organisational change must include a strong focus on individual change.

It should further be noted from Figure 5.1 that within the work context most adults face challenges and situations that are beyond their developmental understanding (indicated as levels of work in the figure). To be effective, the leader's way of thinking and acting must be equal or superior to the complexity of his/her context.[18] What is important for leadership coaching is the awareness that for many leaders the complexity inherent in the context is overwhelming their capacity to cope. In this regard, evidence suggests that less than eight percent of leaders have reached the interdependent stage of development.[19]

Furthermore, emerging practice in leadership development is to align developmental strategies to four proposed levels of *organisational maturity*: *Level 1*: Inconsistent management training; *Level 2*: Structured training according to competency models; *Level 3*: Leadership development and developing the organisation; and *Level 4*: Strategic leadership development where leadership is an integral part of the overall talent management strategy.[20] Leadership coaching is increasingly used as the intervention on Levels 3 and 4.

Given increased application of leadership coaching in organisations, an understanding of the conditions under which coaching is most effective is highly relevant and will be discussed next.

What are the Critical Success Factors for Effective Leadership Coaching Outcomes?

What we do know about coaching outcomes is that in order to increase coaching effectiveness, emphasis should be placed on the attributes of the *coach*, the *coachee* (or client), the organisational *context*, and the coaching *relationship*.[21] In addition, to coach effectively we also need a clear *purpose*, a body of knowledge (or framework) of underlying *perspectives;* and a respectful *process* of working to understand the interrelatedness of all the elements applicable to each stage in the coaching intervention.[ii] Figure 5.2 illustrates the critical elements for effective leadership coaching outcomes, which will be discussed in some detail. Note, however, that all of the elements are equally important and must be in place for a successful coaching outcome to be achieved.

---

ii   Drawing on the concept of case formulation, I find value in the purpose, perspective and process meta-framework introduced by Lane and Corrie (2009) in understanding the issues applicable to each stage in the coaching intervention.

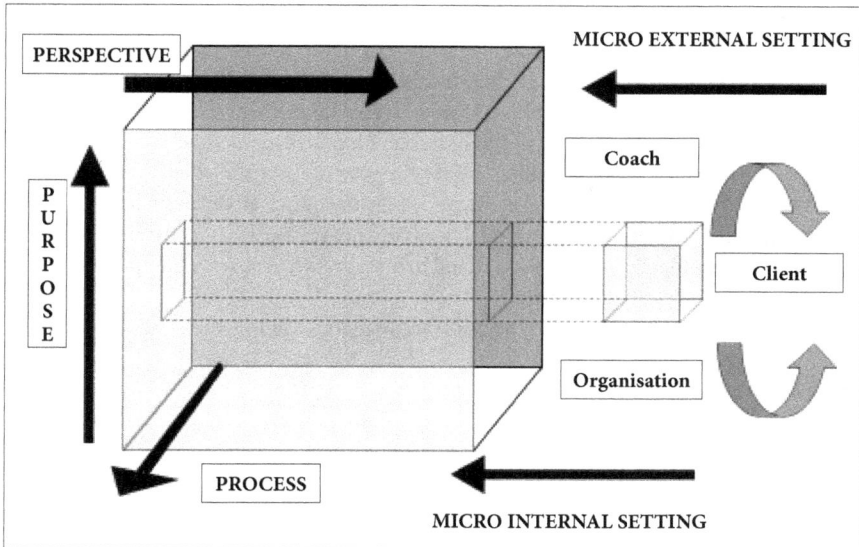

Figure 5.2: Critical elements for successful coaching outcomes[22]
Source: *Lane & Corrie, 2009*[23]

Client needs: Why do clients seek coaching?

From a leadership coaching perspective, I position the client as not only the individual leader (= client) but also the team and broader organisation formally involved in the coaching process. In an attempt to find answers to the question why organisations want their leaders to be coached, Pavur[24] identified the following categories of clients' perceived needs for coaching:

1. *Training and development:* to facilitate self-awareness; to build social skills; align motives and values to the culture of the organisation; and to improve organisational outcomes and performance.
2. *Self-actualisation and well-being:* primarily to promote wellbeing; to support work-life balance; and to improve the quality of life, and work satisfaction and engagement.
3. *Adaptation and resilience:* to interpret ethical challenges; work with complex problems by engaging stakeholders; improve functions in uncertain environments; change organisational culture; prepare for multiple possible futures; and to improve functioning across cultures.

The preceding discussion clearly indicates that what drives the need (or purpose) for coaching is "as the client defines it". It is also aligned with research on executive coaching as a role function[25] that identified the four primary needs of an executive: to learn a new skill; to perform better in current role; to prepare for a future role; and to enable the execution of the executive agenda.

While clients may seek coaching to address a specific need, organisations too have an organisational agenda aligned to retention strategies; performance management; change management; succession planning; and career management,[26] which requires seamless integration within the talent management architecture of the organisation. In addition, each client also brings a specific personality, values, beliefs and experience that influence the readiness to be coached as well as the commitment to the coaching process.

Certainly, organisations also have different levels of readiness and commitment to coaching interventions. Some provide extensive support and resources in an attempt to build a coaching culture and capability within organisations aligned to their strategic business outcomes. Within these organisations the sponsorship of the coaching intervention typically resides with the CEO, with HR taking on the custodian role. In contrast, other organisations may focus only on individual coaching assignments with the client driving the need for coaching.

However, organisations are increasingly recognising that the unique nature of leadership coaching must be able to meet the needs of both the organisation and clients. These needs may be at different developmental or career stages while operating at different levels within the organisation.[27] Individual and organisational needs are not necessarily incompatible. Leadership coaching is therefore ideally positioned to attend to both by means of a flexible and individualised process to achieve the desired outcomes.

Box 5.1 indicates some emerging trends regarding organisational readiness.

Box 5.1: Emerging trends with regard to organisational readiness

---

Organisational readiness

- To appoint a Coaching Manager to oversee the integration of coaching within organisational processes, the selection of coaches, and assisting in coach-client matching.

- Where organisations make use of a pool of internal and external coaches, a Lead Coach or Coaching Supervisor is also appointed. Here the emphasis is on the development of the coach, providing support where required, as well as ensuring that quality standards are adhered to.[iii]

- The management of a coaching engagement is typically on a continuum from totally unmanaged to strongly managed, focusing on aspects such as: assessing an individual's need for coaching; determining readiness for coaching; getting line managers on board; a rigorous coach selection process; matching the coach and client; managing the contracting process; monitoring the effectiveness; and measuring the impact.[iv]

The leadership coach: Leadership coaching requires unique behaviour, knowledge and skills

A leadership coach can be described as: a professionally trained and qualified individual who may or may not have credentials issued by voluntary professional associations, and who provides coaching services to leaders, executives and senior managers with the purpose of improving their leadership effectiveness. A leadership coach therefore excludes a life coach and mentor and must also be differentiated from a counsellor.

However, the question regarding who is best qualified to be a leadership (or executive) coach remains a contentious issue. There are currently two dominant and competing views:

1. Some argue that psychologists are most qualified as a result of their particular training in psychological approaches and adult development, and their use of psychological theory and assessment and skills in building and maintaining confidential and trusting relationships.[28]
2. The opposing view is that coaches must be knowledgeable about the business context in which they operate, with an understanding of leadership, management principles, and organisational culture and politics.[29]

---

iii For a detailed discussion of the role of supervision in organisations, see Koortzen & Odendaal (2016).
iv For a review of different trends in executive coaching, see Odendaal (2009:38–42).

In this chapter I argue that sufficient knowledge and skill of both coaching – grounded in different perspectives that include psychological theory – and leadership theory and practice are essential for effective leadership coaching outcomes.

In selecting a coach, the buyers of the coaching service will also determine whether a leadership or executive coach may be required, or whether an internal coach will be appropriate. Typically, leaders and executives are coached by external coaches and employees by internal coaches.[30] The goal and outcome to be achieved may be similar. However, differences may be observed in coaching relationships. This is especially relevant in coach selection, where the leader will play an active part in the selection process compared to internal coaches that are usually appointed. Depending on the needs of the client and the organisation, specific sets of knowledge, skills and experience may be a prerequisite, such as accreditation for specific assessment tools and techniques.

A further important element to consider is the proficiency level and experience of the coach, as well as individual qualities such as interpersonal skills that should be aligned with a specific coaching approach and style.[31] Several professional coaching associations have clear competency frameworks anchored in specific knowledge bases.[v] Depending on the specific role profile and type of coaching applied, supporting competencies may be quite different and may indeed extend the generic competencies such as: listening, questioning, providing feedback and building relationships. Additional sets of competence required by a leadership coach are: the ability to operate on a specific level of complexity; communicate on all levels; work in a multicultural context supported by intercultural competence; engage with a client at the level of beliefs, emotions, values and meta-cognitive patterns; and address the personal side when coaching for professional and business-related issues.

Coaching relationship

Establishing the relationship is typically the first step in any coaching engagement. From a practice perspective, the quality and strength of the coaching relationship is intuitively perceived as important, highlighting the interdependence between coach and client. Ineffective coach–client relationships were cited as the primary reason in 65% of cases where coaching was terminated.[32]

When matching a coach and client, prominent criteria normally listed by both coaches and clients are the importance they place on the relationship and the ability to work together. Matching can therefore be described as the process of finding a suitable coach who meets the needs of the client. Generally the practice is to select two to three coaches from a list or a pool of acceptable coaches who have been pre-selected by the organisation on the basis of certain criteria. This is typically followed by a "chemistry session", or the opportunity to meet each other to determine "fit".

In reviewing research on the importance of the relationship in coaching, it becomes evident that the strength of the coaching relationship, also referred to as the working alliance between client and coach, is seen as the best predictor of successful coaching outcomes.[33] The coaching relationship – characterised by challenge and support – is furthermore a partnership built on rapport, collaboration, commitment, trust and confidentiality.[34] Therefore, critical for effective coaching is spending time building a strong relationship with a client and understanding the factors that may influence the relationship or even predict a good match.

---

v   For a valuable summary of different coaching competency frameworks, I refer the reader to: *The Standards Australian Handbook for Coaching in Organisations* (2010).

Contextual influences having an impact on coaching effectiveness

The operating context of leadership coaching is indeed a critical element that distinguishes leadership coaching from other types of coaching such as life coaching or sport coaching. Ample references exist in the coaching literature illustrating the importance of understanding the context of coaching, and specifically coaching within organisations. Notwithstanding the recognition of the importance of contextual influences, there is a lack of evidence-based approaches regarding the understanding and even the integration of contextual considerations into the design and delivery of coaching interventions.[35] In particular, the deficient manner in which coaches gather information about the operating context stands in stark contrast to the manner in which they assess and gather information about the individual leader.

There are many different lenses, tools and techniques enabling a coach to understand the context in which the client is embedded. Figure 5.2 illustrates the critical position of contextual influences for successful coaching outcomes. It is important to be aware of not only the immediate business context but also how macro conditions external to the organisation influence micro external and internal organisational conditions:

- *Macro contextual complexities* such as the global financial crisis and the influx of refugees across country borders because of unstable political environments has a direct impact on organisations that operate globally.
- *Different strategies employed by organisations to address leadership development challenges* are not influenced only by macro contextual conditions, but also by micro influences such as regional and national politics, socio-economic challenges, and legislation, as well as the immediate business environment.
- *Increasing complexity and changing demands of the operating context of organisations* therefore create challenges for the coach and client organisation that influence coaching outcomes.

In my personal leadership coaching experience the majority of clients I coached introduced topics that manifested across different sub-systems that required working on multiple levels.

However, of specific importance to leadership coaching is the dynamic interplay between the leader, leadership and culture, specifically culture at a national, organisational and individual level as well as the combined influence on organisational effectiveness. Leadership and culture are socially constructed and seen as a collective and indeed a universal phenomenon.[36] Leadership can therefore be viewed either from a:

- *Universalist approach:* an emphasis on universal leadership traits that are seen as comparable although not equally important across cultures; or from a
- *Culture-specific approach:* an emphasis on different cultures that have different expectations for leadership. Certain leadership behaviour may be unique to a specific culture.

It is therefore important for the leadership coach not only to be cognisant of contextual complexities but also to be aware of one's *personal perspective,* specific knowledge, and understanding used as a basic or specific lens within coaching conversations. Notable challenges for both the coach and client, and including their organisation, are therefore the recognition of cross-cultural differences in leadership because of the differential weighting of variables such as power, relationship orientation, ethics and risk-taking.

Given the increased recognition of the importance of the leader-culture interaction, and the highly diverse and complex South African society, is it imperative for leadership coaches to include a cultural mindset into their practice of coaching and focusing on the development of intercultural competence. To enhance *intercultural competence*, the focus should be on awareness, knowledge and skill for both the coach and client.[37] Evidence points towards the development of *cultural awareness* – the process where culturally relevant information is intellectually processed; and *cultural sensitivity* – the emotional reaction towards an interculturally significant experience.[38]

Box 5.2 provides critical success factors for effective coaching.

Box 5.2: Critical success factors for effective coaching

Critical success factors influencing effective coaching outcomes to be taken into account when planning a coaching intervention[39]

- The behaviour, knowledge and skill of both the coach and the coachee
- The proper matching of coach and coachee
- Ensuring a positive working relationship
- The readiness of the coachee
- Readiness for and support in the organisation for coaching
- The alignment to the business strategy
- A seamless integration of coaching with talent management systems and processes in the organisation
- A recognition of the impact of contextual influences on the coaching relationship and process
- Competence in intercultural interactions

Understanding purpose, perspectives and process for successful coaching outcomes

Next under discussion is the importance of structuring the coaching conversation in such a manner that there is a clear understanding of the *purpose* to be achieved (see Figure 5.2). Any method of information gathering, and tools or techniques utilised in the coaching, must not only support (i) the purpose but also be aligned to (ii) preferred models and theories as well as (iii) the knowledge base and experience of both the coach and client. The *perspectives* from which we operate help us to understand the purpose of coaching engagements and determine the *process* to follow.

Against the backdrop of the above discussion of defining coaching, coaching can be viewed as a process in search of patterns. In the complex world of human experiences there are indeed many possible patterns and different approaches (or perspectives) that can be employed to assist the client to make meaning out of experiences. However, the patterns we detect as leadership coaches depend on the theories, models and assumptions we bring to bear on the coaching relationship and process. Based on the answers to the questions posed in Table 5.2, it is reasonable to assert that regardless of preferred approach, the coach must be able to adapt to the needs and preferred perspective of the client.

Therefore, perspectives of both the coach and client can be viewed as metaphorical lenses we use to filter what is important from what is less important within a specific coaching context. Perspectives are strongly informed by personal values, our beliefs about knowledge and an understanding of what we do well in relation to that knowledge as well as the limits of our competence. Grounded in evidence-based practice, I further support the notion that each practitioner must engage in regular critical and reflective examinations of the purpose, perspective and process he/she is applying in his/her own practice, based on the questions as presented in Table 5.2.

Table 5.2: Applying the Purpose, Perspective and Process model as a framework for case formulation

Case Formulation	Essential elements	Questions the coach must consider
Purpose	Understanding the purpose of the intervention	How did you define the purpose in advance of working with the client?
	Understanding expectations of key stakeholders	Who are the key stakeholders and what are the expectations of each?
	Clarification of the role of each stakeholder	What is the role (with supporting responsibilities) of each stakeholder? What investment is each party expected to make in terms of time, energy and resources?
	Influence of the wider context	What in the broader context (= operating, micro and macro) can influence the purpose of the intervention?
Perspective	Approach from a specific theory, model, and approach: single perspective or proprietary framework	What perspective informs your approach? What perspective informs the client's approach?
	Engagement with client and type of narrative determine the perspective best suited: a multiple or eclectic perspective that can differ from conversation to conversation	What are the beliefs, knowledge, experience and competencies both client and coach bring to the conversation? To what extent is there coherence?
Process	The purpose and perspective inform the process (or structure) for the intervention	What processes (including methods or tools) did you use to meet the purpose within the constraints of the perspectives available to you and the client/organisation? How did you structure the process?

Source: *Compiled from Lane and Corrie (2009)*[40]

The process followed must further be determined by both the purpose of the intervention and how the purpose was defined from a specific perspective. A coaching cycle typically consists of different steps taken to reach the outcomes of the intervention such as: coach-matching, contracting, relationship building, assessment, intervention, reflection, and evaluation.

There are indeed different step-based frameworks available in literature, ranging from two to ten steps, that provide a series of questions to structure the coaching conversation.[vi][41] A popular questioning framework is the GROW model that provides specific questions regarding the *goal*, current *reality*, different *options* and *way forward*.[42] Awareness of the different questioning frameworks is important as coaches must be able to provide consistency between individual coaching sessions and the overall outcomes to be achieved.

It must be noted further that different forms of assessment or data gathering typically inform the majority of coaching processes. Assessments can be based on interviews with the client or other important stakeholders (by means of qualitative 360-degree feedback) or through structured assessment instruments (for example, personality, values, emotional intelligence, and leadership practices, to name a few). Reviewing current leadership coaching practices, it is evident that standardised measures are increasingly applied,[43] with the supporting belief that psychometrically sound measures are a prerequisite for application in a multicultural context. In addition, development centres are also popular methods employed by organisations that include behaviour observations and experiential exercises.

Box 5.3 provides a list of current trends regarding the coaching process.

Box 5.3: Current trends with regard to the coaching process

The coaching process

- In-person coaching is still dominant (individual and team coaching).

- Increased use of technology, especially Skype and telephone coaching.

- Regular structured meetings with fixed-length engagements remain dominant (60 to 90 minutes). However, for leadership and executive coaching, sessions typically extend to 90 minutes.

Next, a short description will be provided of specific coaching and leadership theories that informs different perspectives in coaching.

Areas of Knowledge Relevant to Leadership Coaching

Against the backdrop of the preceding discussion of the interrelatedness between purpose, perspective and process, is it imperative for coaching practitioners to be able to describe to the buyers of their coaching services and to their clients which theories and models shape their coaching practice. However, this is not easy, as coaching as an applied discipline is strongly informed by several theories from psychology, adult and experiential learning, organisation development, and systems theory, to name but a few. Additionally, coaches also enter the coaching industry from a diversity of prior backgrounds such as human resources, training, education, consulting, and management.

A wide range of methodological approaches and educational disciplines therefore informs coaching practices. Coaching is indeed multidisciplinary in nature. In this regard, some of the challenging questions are: Which theories and models shape our coaching practice? How do these fit the range of coaching contexts? What knowledge bases are relevant to leadership coaching?

---

vi   Stout-Rostron (2014) provides a comprehensive summary of questioning frameworks.

Coaching theories

Reviewing well-referenced coaching and coaching psychology books[44] and articles, it is evident that there are several areas of knowledge applicable to coaching. Several books provide excellent summaries of the range of strategies informed by different theoretical approaches available to leadership coaches, as well as on how to translate psychological theory into practical coaching skills. In order to achieve successful coaching outcomes, the overall proposition in this chapter is that a coach must not only be cognisant of the major theories informing coaching but also understand their strengths and weaknesses, as well as situations that are well or poorly suited to each approach. The capacity to apply different approaches to a specific coaching situation is referred to as model agility.[vii] Table 5.3 provides a high-level overview of prominent theories and approaches applied in coaching.

Table 5.3: Coaching models grounded in psychological theory

Main forces in psychology informing coaching	Four prevailing coaching models grounded in psychological theory[45]
Behaviourism that informs behavioural and later cognitive–behavioural approaches to coaching	Clinical model: an emphasis on self-awareness and insight
Psychoanalytic theory that focuses on the influence of the unconscious on individual and group behaviour and systems–psychodynamic approaches that include elements of system theory with its focus on roles and authority	Behaviour model: impact of behaviour on self and others
Person-centred approach aligned to humanistic psychology that is relationship-orientated and aims to facilitate the self-determination of the client towards optimal functioning	Systems model: influence of different systems including organisational context on coaching outcomes
	Social constructionist model: re-author new realities through narratives and social interactions

Coaches can approach a client from a specific theoretical approach; a combination of approaches; or an eclectic use of theory. Theories (or models) of human behaviour provide structure on how coaches will engage with their clients. The development and application of a personal framework of coaching – typically referred to as a coaching model even though it may not meet the rigour of model building in research – is general practice. The eclectic use of coaching theories must be based on a thorough understanding of the theoretical assumptions and guiding beliefs as well as limitations of the different theories that inform one's adopted framework, otherwise it may be perceived as empirically underdeveloped.

Current societal changes further require a stronger focus on values, identity formation, and meaning-making, with a movement away from the focus on goals and problem solving. Stelter[46]

---

vii For a detailed discussion on model agility and its application to a case study, see Kauffman & Hodgetts (2016).

refers to three generations of coaching, where the dialogue in each generation is defined by a different basic perspective.

1. ***First generation coaching:*** Skills and performance coaching with a strong focus on goals.
2. ***Second generation coaching:*** Possible solutions with a future focus. The emphasis is on where the client is now so as to build a bridge towards future aspirations, strongly informed by positive psychology and strength-based approaches.
3. ***Third generation coaching:*** Also referred to as narrative collaborative coaching. The focus is on values and identity work, where the coach and client are working together towards personal and social meaning-making. Meaning-making refers to understanding how *we* and *others* think, feel and act.

Third generation coaching grounded in the social-constructionist paradigm as listed in Tables 45.3 and 45.4 provides a deep and reflective re-connection to a more human and relational way of being. The African concept of *Ubuntu,* anchored in a value system that prioritises relationships,[viii] [47] [48] is particularly well suited as a framework for third generation coaching.

Leadership theories

Leadership coaching additionally requires knowledge, skills and competencies grounded in leadership theory. As different chapters in *Building Leadership Talent* clearly indicate, our collective understanding of leadership and how it develops is continuously evolving. There has been a general movement from leadership residing in a person or role to leadership as an influence and a collective process, with further transition towards shared leadership, including interdependency between individuals, teams and organisations.[49] From this perspective leaders are any person in the organisation actively involved in the process of providing direction, alignment and commitment.[50]

Important in leadership coaching is the notion that the coach, client and organisation must determine what leadership is for them in the specific context they find themselves as well as what constitutes effective and ineffective leadership. An organisation needs to craft a Strategic Leadership Framework to direct and guide its thinking and action regarding leadership.

Leadership identification remains a major area for research and practice. Strong evidence exists to suggest that underlying personality traits should serve as key considerations when assessing leadership potential, in this way determining the psychological capital of a person to meet positional/contextual demands.[51] A notable trend is the movement towards using developmental personality style theory to establish leadership readiness categories to be used during the assessment phase of a coaching relationship. Personality predicts both effective and ineffective leadership. Research evidence provides linkages between personality (dys)functions and leadership style, in particular the impact of "dysfunctional dispositions" and flawed interpersonal behaviours on leader efficacy.[52]

Building on the concept of lenses from which a coach can approach leadership theory, Table 5.4 provides a description of four broad categories of leadership theories based on the research of Bolden and Kirk.[53]

---

viii For an interesting debate about the value of Ubuntu, see Booysen (2015a).

Table 5.4: Broad categories of leadership theories applicable to coaching

> - **Essentialist theories:** a broadly objectivist perspective on leadership grounded in trait, behavioural, situational, contingency and also transformational perspectives. Leadership is presented as strongly grounded in the "qualities of the leader, the behaviours they enact and/or the functions they perform".
>
> - **Relational theories:** the relationships the leader has with others, referred to as "a social influence process" and perceived as a group quality and more inclusive approach to leadership. This approach further recognises how contextual and systemic factors shape leadership practices.
>
> - **Critical theories:** the underlying dynamics of power and politics within organisations. They question "the possibility of the non-existence of leadership as a distinct phenomenon". The emphasis is on dialogues of how leaders can free themselves from control and dependency towards alternative narratives.
>
> - **Constructionist approaches:** a broadly interpretivist perspective where leadership is essentially regarded as a process of sense making and re-negotiation of current realities.

To accelerate effective leadership development, it is important for organisations and leadership coaches to begin integrating evidence from both coaching-specific and leadership-related research with their own expertise, within an understanding of the uniqueness of each client and the operating context.

Current Trends in the Evaluation of Leadership Coaching

Despite the popularity and increased use of leadership coaching as strategy for leadership development, the biggest complaint remains that coaching interventions and outcomes are not regularly evaluated. Evaluation refers specifically to the collection of information to assist different stakeholders to make decisions regarding the value, usefulness and adjustments of training and development activities.[54] Because of the individualised nature of leadership coaching, evaluation holds particular challenges for organisations, as each coaching intervention may be qualitatively different. What further complicates coaching evaluation for the buyers of coaching services is that there are no universally accepted criteria for what constitutes a successful leadership coaching outcome.[ix][55]

Return on Investment (ROI) is often presented as the ultimate measure of the benefit of coaching. A monetary value is calculated by subtracting the actual coast of coaching from the estimated value of coaching, and presenting that as a percentage. There are indeed variations in the formula and how the final percentage is calculated. Notwithstanding variations, coaching and consulting organisations typically report on ROI to market and promote their services. The biggest critique against the use of ROI measures are the fact that input costs may vary (for example, the amount charged by the coach) and that not all variables are controlled (for example, contextual influence, team input).[56] It is furthermore quite difficult to show a specific causal relationship between a coaching intervention and improvements in organisational outcomes.

The focus has therefore shifted to measuring the non-monetary benefits of coaching, such as generic coaching outcomes and utilising engagement frameworks. as well as measurement of Return on Expectations (ROE). Measures of ROE are typically self-evaluations of the ability to achieve goals such as increasing self-confidence or improving interpersonal relationships.

---

ix   Grant et al. (2010) provides a useful overview of the current state of evaluation in coaching.

Because of the intrinsic value that coaching may have for different people, organisations are also starting to use less complicated measures, such as asking clients if they felt the coaching was worth their time; whether it made a positive change; and if they would recommend it to a colleague.[57]

A review of outcomes evaluation studies makes it clear that there are indeed huge variations in coaching outcomes that further influence meaningful comparisons.[58] Typical outcomes measured include leader role efficacy,[59] the relationship processes of rapport, trust and commitment,[60] as well as the coach-client relationship,[61] to mention but a few. These outcomes variables are typically measured as the difference in state before and after coaching as well as across leaders. The use of client-coachee self-ratings only is seen as a huge limitation in the majority of reported outcome evaluation studies.

When determining evaluation criteria one needs to be aware that coaching outcomes may be culture-specific. Some studies revealed national differences in perceptions of effective leadership that may be associated with cultural dimensions, and therefore may impact evaluation outcomes. Notwithstanding challenges experienced in measuring the value of coaching or scepticism about ultimate usefulness, there is an increasing acknowledgement of the unique contribution that evaluation studies can make to enhance decision-making and investment in leadership coaching.

Box 5.4 depicts current trends regarding coaching evaluation research.

Box 5.4: Current trends with regard to coaching evaluation

Coaching evaluation

- Coaching evaluation must take into account the needs of various stakeholders: coach, client, client organisation and coaching organisations.

- Coaching evaluation must focus on *outcomes* (= summative evaluation) to assess effectiveness as a development intervention, and *processes* (= formative evaluation) to account for the dynamic and individualised nature of coaching.

- In the context of leadership coaching, *formative* evaluation focuses on aspects of the client, coach, client-coach relationship, and the coaching process that contribute to the success of the coaching intervention.

- The complexity of the evaluation process is influenced by variation in potential data sources as well as the methodologies applied.

- Organisations are starting to use Return on Expectations (ROE) measures as an alternative to Return on Investment (ROI) as a measure of success.

Conclusion

My chapter departs from the vantage point that leadership coaching can make a significant contribution to the development of leader, leadership and leadership culture in an operating context characterised by volatility, uncertainty, complexity and ambiguity. Leadership coaching as a strategy for vertical development in organisations needs to be informed by a strong emphasis on leadership identity development, in which one moves from an individual to a more relational approach to leadership. It is essential for effective leadership coaching outcomes that sufficient knowledge of the theory and approaches that inform coaching, as well an integration of this knowledge with one's own expertise in practice, in both coaching and leadership, must exist.

Notable trends and practical implications of developments with respect to leadership coaching provide a broad overview that inform practice and guide further research. These trends and developments indicate a shift from conventional leadership development strategies towards vertical development interventions that are increasingly strategic in nature.

Endnotes

1   Mitchell, Ray & Van Ark, 2014; PwC, 2015; Snowden & Boone, 2007; Stacey, 2011.
2   Elliott, 2011; Ladegard & Gjerde, 2014, Stelter, 2014; Sperry, 2013.
3   Theeboom, Beersma & van Vianen, 2013.
4   Loew & Garr, 2011.
5   Elliott, 2011.
6   Barner & Higgins , 2007.
7   Bachkirova, Cox & Clutterbuck, 2014, p. 3; Standards Australia, 2010.
8   Grant et al. 2010, p. 3.
9   Cavanagh, 2006; Kilburg, 2004; Cox, Bachkirova & Clutterbuck, 2014.
10 Grant, Curtayne & Burton, 2009, p. 397.
11 Ladegard & Gjerde, 2014.
12 Clutterbuck & Megginson, 2005.
13 Clarke, 2013; Bolden & Kirk, 2009; Ely et al., 2010; Ladegard & Gjerde, 2014; Odendaal & Le Roux, 2016.
14 Clarke, 2013; Day et al., 2014.
15 Kegan & Lahey, 2009.
16 Bersin & Associates, 2007, 2013; Jaques, 2006; Kegan & Lahey, 2009; Petrie, 2013.
17 Kegan & Lahey, 2009; McGuire & Rhodes, 2009; Petrie, 2013.
18 Jacques, 2006; Stacey, 2011.
19 Rooke & Torbert, 2005.
20 Clarey, Mallon & Vickers, 2012; Lamoureux, 2013; Loew & Garr, 2011.
21 Grant et al., 2010.
22 Lane & Corrie, 2009.
23 Lane & Corrie, 2009.
24 Pavur, 2013, p. 290.
25 Witherspoon & White, 1996
26 Ely, Boyce, Zaccaro & Whyman, 2010.
27 Ely et al., 2010.
28 Grant et al., 2010; Feldman & Lankau, 2005; Sperry, 2013.
29 Ahern, 2003; Grant et al., 2010
30 Spaten & Flensborg, 2013
31 Cox, Bachkirova & Clutterbuck, 2014

32 Tompson et al., 2008.
33 Page & De Haan, 2014.
34 Ely et al., 2010.
35 Nieminen, Biermeier-Hanson & Denison, 2013.
36 Booysen, 2015b; Bennett (2014), House et al., 2004; Hofstede, Hofstede & Minkov, 2010.
37 Bird et al., 2009; DeBoer Kreider (2013).
38 Christiansen et al., 2011; Cox, 2003.
39 Cavanagh & Lane, 2012; Lane & Corrie, 2009.
40 The table was compiled from Lane and Corrie (2009).
41 Stout-Rostron, 2014.
42 Whitmore, 1992; Cox, 2003.
43 Passmore, 2008.
44 Cox, Bachkirova & Clutterbuck, 2014; Palmer & Whybrow, 2007; Passmore, Peterson & Freire, 2013.
45 Barner and Higgins, 2007, p. 149.
46 Stelter, 2014, p. 33.
47 Booysen, 2015a.
48 Geber & Keane, 2013.
49 Day & Harrison, 2007; Petrie, 2013.
50 McCauley & Van Velsor, 2004.
51 Best, 2010; Nelson & Hogan, 2009; Sperry, 2008.
52 Nelson & Hogan, 2009; Sperry, 2008; Wasylyshyn, Shorey & Chaffin, 2012.
53 Bolden & Kirk, 2009, p. 71.
54 Ely et al., 2010.
55 Ely et al., 2010; Ladegard & Gjerde, 2014.
56 Grant et al., 2010.
57 DiGirolama, 2015, based on a White Paper series between ICF and SHRM.
58 Ely et al., 2010; Grant et al., 2010; Ladegard & Gjerde, 2014.
59 Ladegard & Gjerde, 2014.
60 Boyce, Jackson & Neal, 2010.
61 Baron, Morin & Morin, 2011.

References

Ahern, G. 2003. 'Designing and implementing coaching/mentoring competencies: A case study'. *Counselling Psychology Quarterly*, 16(4):373–383.

Bachkirova, T, Cox, E & Clutterbuck, D. 2014. 'Introduction'. In E Cox, T Bachkirova & D Clutterbuck (eds). *The complete handbook of coaching*. 2nd ed. London, UK: Sage Publications, Inc. 1–20.

Barner, R & Higgins, J. 2007. 'Understanding implicit models that guide the coaching process'. *Journal of Management Development*, 26(2):148–158.

Baron, L, Morin, L & Morin, D. 2011. 'Executive coaching'. *Journal of Management Development*, 30(9):847–864.

Bersin & Associates Industry Report (September 2007). High-impact leadership development: Best Practices, vendor profiles and Industry solutions. Research Bulletin by Kim Lamoureux, Bersin by Deloitte. Retrieved: www.bersin.com/library.

Best, KC. 2010. 'Assessing leadership readiness using developmental personality style: A tool for leadership coaching'. *International Journal of Evidence Based Coaching and Mentoring*, 8(1):22–33.

Bird, A, Mendenhall, M, Stevens, MJ & Oddou, G. 2009. 'Defining the content domain of intercultural competence for global leaders'. *Journal of Managerial Psychology*, 25(8):810–828.

Bolden, R & Kirk, P. 2009. 'African leadership: Surfacing new understandings through leadership development', *International Journal of Cross Cultural Management*, 9(1):69–86, April. 71.

Booysen, LAE. 2015a. 'The two faces of Ubuntu – an inclusive positive or exclusive parochial leadership perspective?' In L Morgan-Robert, L Wooten & M Davidson (eds). *Positive organizing in a global society: Understanding and engaging differences for capacity-building and inclusion*. New York, NY: Taylor & Francis Group.

Booysen, LAE. 2015b. 'Cross-cultural coaching' (Ch 10). In D Riddle, E Hoole & E Gullette (eds). *Center for creative leadership handbook of coaching in organizations*. San Francisco, CA: Jossey-Bass. 241-288.

Boyce, LA, Jackson, J & Neal, L. 2010. 'Building successful leadership coaching relationships: Examining the impact of matching criteria in a leadership coaching program'. *Journal of Management Development*, 29(10):914–931.

Cavanagh, M. 2006. 'Coaching from a systemic perspective: A complex adaptive conversation'. In D Stober & AM Grant (eds). *Evidence-based coaching handbook*. New Jersey, NJ: Wiley. 313–354.

Cavanagh, M & Lane, D. 2012. 'Coaching psychology coming of age: The challenges we face in the messy world of complexity'. *International Coaching Psychology Review*, 7(1):75–90.

Christiansen, AT, Thomas, V, Kafescioglu, N, Karakurt, G, Lowe, W, Smith, W, *et al.* 2011. 'Multicultural supervision: Lessons learned about an ongoing struggle'. *Journal of Marital and Family Therapy*, 37(1):109–119.

CIPD. 2015. *Learning and development survey 2015*. [Online]. Available: http://www.cipd.co.uk/learninganddevelopmentsurvey. [Accessed 1 June 2016].

Clarey, J, Mallon, D & Vickers, M. 2012. *Leadership of the high-impact learning organisation*. Bersin & Associates. [Online]. Available: http://www.bersin.com/library. [Accessed 1 June 2016].

Clarke, N. 2013. 'Model of complexity leadership development'. *Human Resource Development International*, 16(2):135–150.

Clutterbuck, D. & Megginson, D. (2005). *Making Coaching Work: Creating a Coaching Culture*. London: CIPD.

Cox, E. 2003. 'The contextual imperative: Implications for coaching and mentoring'. *International Journal of Evidence Based Coaching and Mentoring*, 1(1):9–22.

Cox, EE, Bachkirova, T & Clutterbuck, D. 2014. 'Theoretical traditions and coaching genres: Mapping the Territory'. *Advances in Developing Human Resources*, 16(2):139–160.

Day, DV & Harrison, MM. 2007. 'A multilevel, identity-based approach to leadership development'. *Human Resource Management Review*, 17(4):360–373.

Day, DV, Fleenor, JW, Atwater, LE, Sturm, RE & McKee, RA. 2014. 'Advances in leader and leadership development: A review of 25 years of research and theory'. *The Leadership Quarterly*, 25(1):63–82.

DiGirolama, J. 2015. 'Coaching for professional development'. *SHRM-SIOP science of HR white paper series*. New York, NY: Oxford University Press.

Elliott, R. 2011. 'Utilising evidence-based leadership theories in coaching for leadership development: Towards a comprehensive integrating conceptual framework'. *International Coaching Psychology Review*, 6(1):46–70.

Ely, K, Boyce, LA, Nelson, JK, Zaccaro, SJ, Hernez-Broome, G, & Whyman, W. 2010. 'Evaluating leadership coaching: A review and integrated framework'. *The Leadership Quarterly*, 21(4):585–599.

Feldman, DC & Lankau, MJ. 2005. 'Executive coaching: A review and agenda for future research'. *Journal of Management*, 31(6):829–848.

Geber, H & Keane, M. 2013. 'Extending the worldview of coaching research and practice in Southern Africa: The concept of ubuntu'. *International Journal of Evidence Based Coaching and Mentoring*, 11(2):8–17.

Grant, AM, Curtayne, L & Burton, G. 2009. 'Executive coaching enhances goal attainment, resilience and workplace well-being: A randomized controlled study'. *The Journal of Positive Psychology*, 4(5):396–407.

Grant, AM, Passmore, J, Cavanagh, MJ & Parker, H. 2010. 'The state of play in coaching today: A comprehensive review of the field'. *International Review of Industrial and Organizational Psychology*, 25:125–167.

Hofstede, G, Hofstede, GJ & Minkov, M. 2010. *Cultures and organizations: Software of the mind.* 3rd ed. New York, NY: McGraw Hill.

House, RJ, Hanges, PJ, Javidan, M, Dorfman, PW & Gupta, V. 2004. *Culture, leadership and organizations: The GLOBE study of 62 societies.* Thousand Oaks, CA: Sage Publications, Inc.

Hughes, PD & Campbell, A. 2009. *Learning and Development Outlook 2009: Learning in Tough Times.* Ottawa, ON: Conference Board of Canada.

Inman, AG & DeBoer Kreider, E. 2013. 'Multicultural competence: Psychotherapy practice and supervision'. *Psychotherapy*, 50(3):346–350.

Jacques, E. 2006. *Requisite organization: A total system for effective managerial organization and managerial leadership for the 21st century.* 2nd rev. ed. Baltimore, MD: Cason Hall & Co. Publishers.

Kauffman, C & Hodgetts, WH. 2016. 'Model agility: Coaching effectiveness and four perspectives on a case study'. *Consulting Psychology Journal: Practice and Research*, 62(2):157–176.

Kegan, R & Lahey, L. 2009. *Immunity to change: How to overcome it and unlock potential in yourself and your organization.* Boston, MA: Harvard Business School Press.

Kilburg, RR. (2004. 'When shadows fall: Using psychodynamic approaches in executive coaching'. *Consulting Psychology Journal: Practice and Research*, 56(4):246–268.

Koortzen, P & Odendaal, A. 2016. 'Coaching supervision: Towards a systemic coaching supervision framework'. In LE Van Zyl, MW Stander & A Odendaal (eds). *Coaching psychology: Meta-theoretical perspectives and applications in multi-cultural contexts.* New York, NY: Springer. 67–96.

Ladegard, G & Gjerde, S. 2014. 'Leadership coaching, leader role efficacy, and trust in subordinates. A mixed methods study assessing leadership coaching as a leadership development tool'. *The Leadership Quarterly*, 25(4):631–646.

Lamoureux, K. 2013. 'Five trends in levering leadership development to drive a competitive advantage'. *Bersin by Deloitte Research Bulletin*, 7 March. Oakland, CA: Deloitte Development LLC. [Online]. Available: https://www.bersin.com/Practice/Detail.aspx?id=16296. [Accessed 1 June 2016].

Lane, DA & Corrie, S. 2009. 'Does coaching psychology need the concept of formulation?' *International Coaching Psychology Review*, 4(2):195–208.

Loew, L & Garr, S. 2011. *High-impact leadership development: Driving organizational maturity and business impact.* [Online]. Available: https://www.bersin.com/Practice/Detail.aspx?id=14449. [Accessed 1 June 2016].

McCauley, C & Van Velsor, E. 2004. *The Center for Creative Leadership Handbook of Leadership Development.* San Francisco, CA: Jossey-Bass.

McGuire, C & Rhodes, G. 2009. *Transforming your leadership culture.* San Francisco, CA: Jossey-Bass.

Mitchell, C, Ray, RC & Van Ark, B. 2014. *Creating opportunity out of adversity: Building innovative, people-driven organizations.* Corporate Conference Board. [Online]. Available: https://www.conference-board.org/retrievefile.cfm?filename=TCB_1570_15_RR_CEO_Challenge3.pdf&type=subsite. [Accessed 1 June 2016].

Nelson, E & Hogan, R. 2009. 'Coaching on the dark side'. *International Coaching Psychology Review*, 4(1):9–21.

Nieminen, L, Biermeier-Hanson, B & Denison, D. 2013. 'Aligning leadership and organizational culture: The leader–culture fit framework for coaching organizational leaders'. *Consulting Psychology Journal: Practice and Research*, 65(3):177–198.

Odendaal, A. 2009. *Executive coaching.* Executive Thought Leadership Briefing. Department of Industrial Psychology and People Management. Johannesburg, ZA: University of Johannesburg. 38-42.

Odendaal, A & Le Roux, A-R. 2016. 'Contextualising coaching psychology within multi-cultural contexts'. In LE Van Zyl, MW Stander & A Odendaal (eds). *Coaching psychology: Meta-theoretical perspectives and applications in multi-cultural contexts.* New York, NY: Springer, pp. 3–25.

Page, N & De Haan, E. 2014. 'Does executive coaching work? *The Coaching Psychologist*, 27(8):582–586.

Palmer, S & Whybrow, A. 2007. *Handbook of coaching psychology: A guide for practitioners.* Hove, UK: Routledge.

Passmore, J. (ed). 2008. *Psychometrics in coaching.* London, UK: Kogan Page.

Passmore, J, Peterson, D & Freire, T. 2013. *Wiley-Blackwell handbook of the psychology of coaching and mentoring.* Oxford, UK: John Wiley.

Pavur, EJ, Jr. 2013. 'Why do organizations want their leaders to be coached? *Consulting Psychology Journal: Practice and Research*, 65(4):289–293.

Petrie, N. 2013. *Vertical leadership development – Part 1: Developing leaders for a complex world.* Center for Creative Leadership. [Online]. Available: http://insights.ccl.org/wp-content/uploads/2015/04/VerticalLeadersPart1.pdf. [Accessed 1 June 2016].

PwC. 2015. *18th Annual global ceo survey.* [Online]. Available: http://www.pwc.com/gx/en/ceo-agenda/ceosurvey/2015.html. [Accessed 1 June 2016].

Rooke, D & Torbert, WR. 2005. 'Seven transformations of leadership'. *Harvard Business Review*, 1-12, April.

Snowden, DJ & Boone, ME. 2007). 'A leader's framework for decision making'. *Harvard Business Review*, 1–8, November.

Spaten, OM & Flensborg, W. 2013. 'When middle managers are doing employee coaching'. *International Coaching Psychology Review*, 8(2):18–39.

Sperry, L. 2008. 'Executive coaching: An intervention, role function, or profession?' *Consulting Psychology Journal: Practice and Research*, 4(1):33–37.

Sperry, L. 2013. 'Executive coaching and leadership assessment: Past, present and future'. *Consulting Psychology Journal, Practice and Research*, 65(4):284–288.

Stacey, R. 2011. *Strategic management and organisational dynamics: The challenge of complexity to ways of thinking about organisations.* 6th ed. New York, NY: Financial Times/Prentice Hall.

Standards Australia. 2010. *Guidelines for coaching in organisations.* Sydney, AUS: SAI Global Limited, under licence from Standards Australia Limited.

Stelter, R. 2014. 'Third generation coaching: Reconstructing dialogues through collaborative practice and a focus on values'. *International Coaching Psychology Review*, 9(1):33–48.

Stout-Rostron, S. 2014. *Business coaching international: Transforming individuals and organizations.* London, UK: Carnac Books.

Theeboom, T Beersma, B & van Vianen, AEM. 2013. 'Does coaching work? A meta-analysis on the effects of coaching on individual level outcomes in an organizational context'. *The Journal of Positive Psychology*, 9(1):1–18.

Tompson, HB, Bear, DJ, Dennis, DJ, Vickers, M, London, J & Morrison, CL. 2008. *Coaching: A global study of successful practices. Trends and future possibilities 2008–2018.* New York, NY: AMACOM (publishing division of the American Management Association). [Online]. Available: http://www.amanet.org/training/articles/Coaching-A-Global-Study-of-Successful-Practices-02.aspx. [Accessed 1 June 2016].

Wasylyshyn, KM, Shorey, HS & Chaffin, JS. 2012. 'Patterns of leadership behaviour: Implications for successful executive coaching outcomes'. *The Coaching Psychologist*, 8(2):74–85.

Whitmore, J. 1992. *Coaching for performance.* London, UK: Nicholas Brealey.

Witherspoon, R & White, R. P. 1997. *Four essential ways that coaching can help executives.* Greensboro, NC: Center for Creative Leadership.

SECTION 4

LEADERSHIP DEVELOPMENT INSTITUTIONS

Chapter 6

BUSINESS SCHOOLS AS HUBS OF LEADERSHIP EDUCATION

Piet Naudé

Business Schools present themselves as places where "leadership"[i] is taken seriously. Paging through a recent edition of *The Economist* (27 February to 4 March 2016),[1] the advertising section included top business schools recruiting students with tag-lines such as "There is no glass ceiling to your leadership potential"; and reference was made to "Realising superior" where one will be enabled "to create sustainable advantage".

In most business schools, "leadership" is included as a core module in formal education and forms the basis of many courses in executive education. In South Africa we have the example of Unisa (the University of South Africa), which calls its flagship business school degree the Masters in Business **Leadership** (MBL) – probably to emphasise that business education is more than being a master in just the **administration** of business, as is assumed by the commonly used "MBA" designation.

The purpose of this chapter deals with the wish of business schools to be centres for "leadership education". If business schools want to live up to this claim there are at least four areas of application that could cumulatively assist in verifying the claim, and they are the topics addressed in this chapter: (i) self-leadership; (ii) academic leadership; (iii) executive leadership education; and (iv) leading public discourse.

"Self-leadership" of Business Schools[ii]

For the purpose of this discussion the concept of self-mastery or self-leadership is extended from a personal perspective and applied to an institutional setting. Against this backdrop, it can be stated that there is no guarantee that business schools apply to themselves what they teach others. There are at least two reasons for this:

- **Firstly:** Public business schools are usually part of a university, and they consequently function in the "iron cage" (Weber) of hierarchical administration processes, subject to national education policies and oversight. In essence, these business schools function as a subdivision of the public sector. Despite the nominal autonomy of universities and the "distance" between public business schools and faculties of commerce, a bureaucratic spirit invades the administration of affairs – from HR to finance to student recruitment. And before one realises that it is happening, one becomes slow and cumbersome when attempting to solve a relatively simple problem, leaving the efficiencies and focus of a business mindset behind.
- **Secondly:** Business school staff rarely, if ever, turn their academic knowledge "inward". The professor of marketing rarely makes input into building the reputation of the school; the professor of finance rarely assists in designing new financial governance systems;

---

i   Other chapters in this book will look at different "definitions" and "styles" of leadership. In this chapter leadership is use in a very rudimentary sense, namely the exercise of social influence by initiating and guiding others. See Manning & Curtis (2015:2–13, 558).

ii For a recent discussion on the link between self-discovery and development of organisational culture in a coaching context, see Van Coller-Peter (2015:1–22).

the professor of entrepreneurship rarely assists the school to be innovative and ahead of market trends; the professors of strategy and future studies can assist corporates, but do not normally play significant roles in charting the trends in business education and designing appropriate responses.

"Self-leadership" for public business schools therefore implies the ability to retain the important academic link to the degree-awarding and funding university while balancing that with negotiated space to take optimal decisions in an agreed devolution of power. This may well mean that precedents are to be created within the university governance system. It further requires the application of internal knowledge in functional disciplines to the institution, culture and operations of the school itself.

This is not a plea to become "inward-looking". It is a plea for self-leadership that utilises readily available insights to the benefit of the school, while recognising the limitations of subjectivity and, perhaps, conflicts of interest.

It is only if a business school is seen as being successfully led **as a business school**, that its claims to educate others in leadership will be credible.

Academic Leadership

Academic leadership in the narrow sense of the word relates to the staff, curriculum and research of a business school. Let us discuss each of these in turn.

Staff

The leadership credibility and authenticity[iii] of staff members working in a business school is determined by a combination of their theoretical knowledge and demonstrated business leadership practices. In an ordinary university department, an academic can go very far with demonstrating theoretical capabilities via conference proceedings and publications. But in a business school – teaching to post-experience students who are in the trenches of business every day – academic staff must be able to relate the theory with practice, preferably not only via case studies, but via their own experiences.

This puts business schools in difficult waters when it comes to appointment and promotion criteria. A senior business person may apply to make a late career change to the academy. She has, for example, a Master's degree or a professional qualification such as Law, Accounting or Engineering. She would fit the leadership profile of the school, but – if appointed – may be pitched at lecturer or senior lecturer level as a result of the bias built into the criteria that work very well for "ordinary" appointments.

The best that business schools can do, is to mix their full-time staff with short-term appointments so that – seen from the perspective of the student – there is a leadership credibility in the classroom.

---

iii Read Manning & Curtis (2015:164–165) for a discussion of authentic leadership.

Curriculum

There are least three ways in which business schools can give prominence to leadership in the curriculum.

The *first option* is to create stand-alone full qualifications such as a post-graduate diploma or an Honours degree in Leadership. The *second option* is to embed the theme of leadership optimally across the curriculum of, for example, the MBA. It requires careful and co-ordinated planning to make sure that leadership in marketing, strategy, finance, and so forth, are addressed in a coherent way so that the student progresses in leadership knowledge and practice as he/she progresses through the different modules. A *third option* is to create a leadership module that runs parallel to the other disciplines. In other words, a concurrent "lane" is created that culminates in an integrated, capstone module towards the end of the qualification.

Assessment is determined by curriculum outcomes. It therefore seems opportune that "assessing" leadership should include a good mix of theory (test, examination), self-reflection (making journal entries), and demonstrated application in the real world of business (case study report).

Research

It is impossible to claim that a business school is a hub for leadership education if it is not supported by credible creation of new knowledge and/or the new application of existing knowledge in the field of leadership. Two observations may assist us in profiling research:

- **Firstly**, "Leadership" is not a distinct discipline such as Economics or Psychology. One could call "leadership studies" a regional knowledge field in the same class as Environmental Studies, Development Studies, or Gender Studies. This by definition requires cross- and post-disciplinary co-operation that may take on any form that the participants collectively bring to the table. Leadership studies therefore by nature require team-research, and we know how rare it is for academics from outside the Natural Sciences to engage in this kind of work.
- **Secondly**, Leadership Studies demonstrate very well what Gibbons and others have called mode 2-knowledge.[2] The old distinction between "theory" and "practice" does not hold water, as problems that arise in practice are the research material for theory from where the new knowledge is tested and applied in practice – creating a virtuous hermeneutical spiral.[iv] Thus, the old question as to whether business schools do "primary" or "applied" research has been superseded.[v]

These two research factors make business schools – and the intellectual leadership potential of the post-graduate students that study there – ideal places to advance our knowledge of leadership and to demonstrate actual leadership in the context of business.

---

iv The metaphor of a "spiral" creates a more "open-ended" process than the traditional idea of a hermeneutical "circle" (stemming from existentialist philosopher, Martin Heidegger) that attempts to express the reciprocal relation between a text (or cultural object) and its reader. See Heidegger (1962:85–89).

v This distinction has even led to the construction of different types of higher education institutions, namely the research university versus the technical university. Read Graham (2013:5–22).

Executive Leadership Education

Executive education is where the tyre of the academy proverbially hits the tar of the business world.

In open enrolment programmes at different levels and of different duration, the theme of leadership should feature prominently. Here the focus is on direct translation and applicability of leadership insights into the business context.

As businesses become cost-conscious and look beyond generic development of their staff, there has been a growth in customised programmes. Here the current or future "leadership gaps" are identified; interventions are designed specifically to fill those gaps; and the programme is presented on-site or for a closed participant group at the business school. Again, the level and duration of the programme can vary widely from basic leadership to executive and global leadership.

Because of constrained staff capacity, most business schools make use of industry experts as contract faculty in executive education. In practice, business schools use their executive education divisions as convening spaces of suitably qualified people.

If one adds the formal leadership qualifications to the wide spread of executive education across industries and across national and international borders, business schools can rightly be viewed as crucial institutions to develop business leadership. In South Africa, the number of people who participated in executive education presented by business schools in 2014 is estimated at 64 441. According to Global Silicon Valley Advisors, a US educational consultancy, corporate and public spending on various forms of external learning will reach $524 billion by 2018.[3]

Public Discourse

The business of business leadership is not confined to business.[vi] Business schools function in a broader society from which they gain their support and legitimacy, and to which they are required to contribute. There are – broadly speaking – three possible scenarios for the relation between business schools and society at large:[vii]

- The *first model* is built on the narrow assumption that the contribution of business schools to society is via the students they educate. These students return to their business and civil life and – because they have been influenced to become more effective leaders – they change the context for the better. The task of the school is therefore to focus on the best possible business education and not to become distracted by broader societal issues. In fact, to venture into broader issues, the school acts outside its mandate and contrary to the reason why it is funded by the state or being paid for by clients.
- The *second model* is built on the assumption that business schools – especially public ones – are already part of society, and have a broader task than merely teaching students or doing research. A business school therefore has to interpret its own context[viii] and then decide how it will become involved. Its social interaction beyond students and clients is required

---

vi This is an obvious allusion to the well-known view defended by Friedman that the business of a business is business. See Friedman (1970).

vii I draw here on the work of Cloete et al. (2001), especially pp. 39–60, where "university connectedness" is discussed.

viii For a very interesting discussion on the intricate link between an organisation and its context, read Veldsman (2015:63–83). For a reflection on the African character of business schools, read Naudé (2015:20–23).

in a situation of grave poverty, high social conflict, or the erosion of democracy. Social activism – in a variety of forms – is accordingly an integral part of the business school's mission, thereby transcending the traditional notion that business and politics do not mix.

- The ***third model*** attempts to combine elements of the two previous models: it agrees with model 1 that the primary task of a business school is academic and business education. However, it disagrees that this education is the only contribution to society. It agrees with the third model that business schools have a broader societal responsibility. However, except in extreme situations, this responsibility is best exercised via the nature and strengths of the business school as an educational institution.

A business school is not a single-issue NGO; nor is it a political party. It does, however, have a responsibility to use its knowledge and resources for the public good. This may indeed include training entrepreneurs in a township environment or providing *pro bono* financial and governance training to NGOs. These kinds of social interventions confirm business schools' institutional identity and can be integrated into the primary tasks of teaching and research, so that the interventions are not perceived as optional extras or philanthropy.

An under-estimated and under-utilised public function of business schools is to act as convening agents for bringing, for example, government and business or business and labour together in a non-partisan space to create greater policy consensus. Business schools should be self-critical enough that they can influence the often ideological space of economic discourse. While one should acknowledge that "facts" or "economic consequences" of pending legislation are theory-laden and social constructs[ix] in themselves, business schools have the potential to play a decisive role to move towards evidence-based policy formulation. If the best available data suggest that power-generation via a single state-owned utility will simply not be adequate without co-operating with private initiatives in "green" technologies; or if the overwhelming evidence is that a 100%-state-owned airline simply does not work; or if research suggests that private healthcare spirals out of cost control, there must be space to engage beyond the ideology of "state-driven" economic growth or the other ideology that "all-out privatisation" is the answer to all problems.

Conclusion

Business schools claim to be hubs of leadership. The burning question is whether they fulfil their potential as credible hubs of leadership knowledge and education. It was argued in this chapter that this question may be answered insofar as business schools demonstrate self-leadership, engage in academic leadership studies and research, present effective leadership training via executive education, and understand their broader leadership role in society.

Endnotes

1   *The Economist*, 2016.
2   Gibbons et al., 1994.
3   Dan Pontefract, 2015.

---

ix One of the classic academic references for the social and constructivist nature of knowledge remains Berger & Luckmann (1966). I also give credence to the well-known Kuhn (1962) for an insight into the paradigm-dependence of knowledge, which explains the difficulty in transcending the intellectual hold of "normal science" on a community of science practitioners.

References

Berger, P & Luckmann, T. 1966. *The social construction of reality. A treatise in the sociology of knowledge*. New York, NY: Random House.

Cloete, N, Bailey, T, Pillay, P, Bunting I & Maassen, P. 2001. *Universities and economic development in Africa*. Wynberg, Cape Town, ZA: Council for Higher Education and Training (CHET).

Friedman, M. 1970. 'The social responsibility of business is to increase its profits'. *The New York Times Magazine*, 13 September.

Gibbons, M, Limoges, C, Nowotny, H, Schwartzman, S, Scott, P & Trow, M. 1994. *The new production of knowledge: The dynamics of science and research in contemporary societies*. London, UK: Sage Publications, Inc.

Graham, G. 2013. 'The university: A critical comparison of three ideal types'. *Kagisano*, 9:5–22, March. Also in R Sugden, M Valania & JR Wilson (eds). *Leadership and cooperation in academia. Reflecting on the roles and responsibilities of university faculty and management*. Cheltenham, UK: Edward Elgar Publishing.

Heidegger, M. 1962. *Being and time*. New York, NY: Harper & Row.

Kuhn, T. 1962. *The structure of scientific revolutions*. Chicago, IL: Chicago University Press.

Manning, G & Curtis, K. 2015. *The art of leadership*. 5th ed. New York, NY: McGraw Hill.

Naudé, P. 2015. 'What does it mean to be an "African" business school?' *Global Focus. The EFMD Business Magazine*, 9(3):20–23. Brussels, BE: European Foundation for Management Development (EFMD).

Pontefract, D. 2015. 'Going back to school with a corporate MBA program'. *Forbes*, 5 August. Jersey City, NJ: Forbes Media LLC. [Online]. Available: http://www.forbes.com/sites/danpontefract/2015/08/05/going-back-to-school-with-a-corporate-mba-program/#59002f01608b. [Accessed 1 August 2016].

The Economist. 27 February to 4 March 2016). 'Really?' *The Economist*, pp. 73–74.

Van Coller-Peter, S. 2015. *Coaching leadership teams*. Randburg, ZA: Knowres Publishing.

Veldsman, TH. 2015. 'The power of the fish is in the water'. *African Journal of Business Ethics*, 9(1):63–83.

Chapter 7

CORPORATE UNIVERSITIES
Philipp Kolo, Rainer Strack & Jens Baiers

As talent becomes the primary source of competitive advantage, organisations must excel at attracting, developing and retaining the talent they need. Corporate universities are emerging as a major vehicle to confront shrinking talent pools and to build strategically critical skills such as digital capabilities.

The engine of economic growth is shifting from financial to human capital. In the past, capital-intensive physical assets drove competitive advantage in many sectors of the industrialised world. Today, the sources of advantage are changing quickly from plants and machines to the people who make organisations work. In this post-industrial society, talent scarcity is looming as the next major organisational challenge.

In the coming years organisations will face a greying workforce; the high expectations of Generation Y; globalisation's unique demands on leadership; and growing employability gaps in emerging markets. Corporate universities are emerging as a powerful vehicle to surmount these challenges. Let us explore these trends and find out how corporate universities can be used to address these trends:

- *A greying workforce:* By 2050, the dependency ratio of those 65 and older will more than double in most G7 countries and in the BRICS nations (= Brazil, Russia, India, China, and South Africa).[i] With the exception of India, these societies will be "greyer" than even Japan, currently the country with the oldest population.[1] Although many organisations face an ageing workforce, few offer lifelong learning opportunities to keep skills current. Corporate universities are primed for this role.

- *Generation Y's expectations:* Many in this generation place a higher value on development opportunities than they do on cash bonuses.[2] Lack of development opportunities is the major reason given by Generation Y employees for leaving an organisation.[3] Corporate universities are turning their attention to attracting and developing the members of this generation.

- *Globalisation's demands on leadership:* As dispersed global operations integrate, leaders must have keen cross-cultural skills and the ability to adapt. Corporate universities have a track record in developing global leadership skills and creating a culture of common values across borders. Equally important, corporate universities are becoming strategy partners in developing the talent, skills, and behaviours needed to drive strategy creation and execution.

- *Emerging market employability gaps:* In the BRICS and many other emerging countries, the percentage of prospective employees with sufficient education and skills, especially in middle management, will be a fraction of what is needed. In a 2012 study, we found that only 15 to 30 percent of university graduates in the BRICS countries are immediately employable.[4] Corporate universities are stepping in to fill the emerging market skills gap.

Supported by professional organisations and certification programmes, corporate universities have been on the rise for decades. In the United States alone, their ranks doubled between 1997 and 2007, from 1 000 to 2 000. Worldwide, there are estimated to be more than 4 000 organisations with formal corporate universities.[5]

---

i   The dependency ratio is the population aged 65 and over divided by the working population (aged 15 to 65).

The growth of corporate universities reflects significant corporate training and development commitments. In 2012, for example, the Boston Consulting Group (BCG) estimated that organisations in the G20 countries had invested nearly $400 billion in training. These investments have been driven mainly by a few developed countries such as the United States, Germany, and France. However, investments in China and India are expected to grow in the wake of employability gaps.

Capital markets are rewarding these investments. In our 2012 global HR research study of nearly 4 300 executives in more than 100 countries, we found that organisations known as "people companies" had delivered higher returns to shareholders and had outperformed their industry's average in eight of the previous ten years. Investments in training also translate into revenue: organisations with strong capabilities in leadership development, talent management, and performance management experienced revenue growth up to 3.5 times higher than the average, and their profit margins ran as high as 2.1 times the average.[6] These people-organisation capabilities lie at the heart of what corporate universities provide.

BCG conducted a global study that included in-depth interviews with senior executives at organisations ranging in size from 8 000 to 300 000 employees in a wide variety of industries. We also conducted interviews with faculty members' representatives from two major academic institutions. Based on this study, the purpose of our chapter is to discuss the critical role of corporate universities as an engine to build human capital.[7] To this end, the six building blocks of the successful corporate university will be discussed, from which seven key success factors will be extrapolated. Our chapter will conclude with some practical questions as guidelines to organisations aspiring to establish their own corporate universities.

The Six Building Blocks Forming the Foundation of Successful Corporate Universities

We identified six strategic building blocks that form the foundation of a successful corporate university. These building blocks are shown in Figure 7.1.

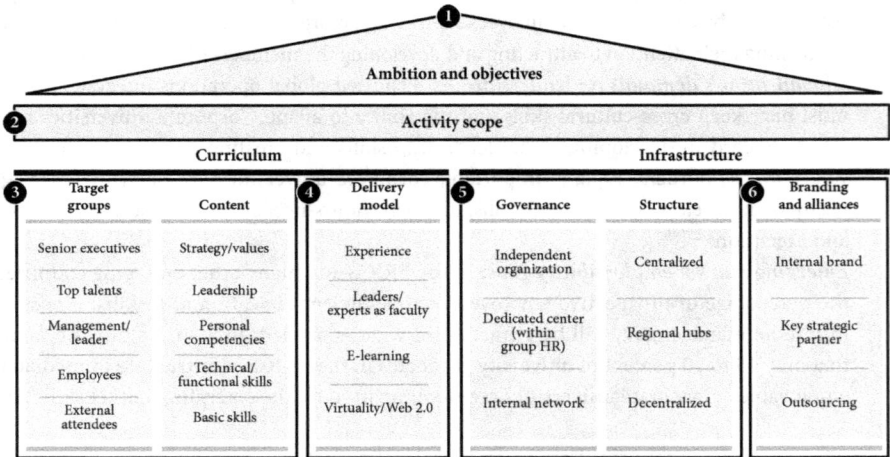

Figure 7.1: *The major building blocks making up a corporate university*

Source: *Expert interviews; BCG analysis, 2013 by The Boston Consulting Group, Inc.*

According to Figure 7.1, a holistic approach to a corporate university comprises six building blocks:

1. ***Ambition and Objectives:*** distilling the purpose and vision of the corporate university
2. ***Activity Scope:*** building a structure to realise the corporate university's strategic role and vision
3. ***Target Audience and Content:*** designing high level curricula for each constituency
4. ***Delivery Model:*** providing a learning environment that supports the corporate university's needs
5. ***Governance and Structure:*** managing reporting relationships, finances, and facilities
6. ***Branding and Alliances:*** creating a strong brand for the corporate university and forging new partnership pathways.

Building Block 1: Ambitions and Objectives

In the past, corporate universities have focused on training design and delivery. Now their role is expanding to support overall organisational strategy and culture. Although corporate universities define themselves in different ways, we have found that they are generally dedicated units acting as partners with senior leadership to develop strategic skills and capabilities. They serve as platforms for strategy development and execution.

Across the board, the executives we interviewed cited two important reasons to develop a corporate university:

*   ***Tying leadership development to organisational strategy:*** Developing talent and leadership is the most important objective (22% of executives). Building a common corporate culture and identity was considered important by 16%. Promoting the company's culture across borders was critical to 12%.
*   ***Supporting strategy development:*** Creating networks and opportunities to develop and disseminate strategic direction was central to 14% of the interviewed executives. Developing a platform for the agenda of the CEO and the board of directors was cited by 10%.

Building Block 2: Activity Scope

Primary roles

Corporate universities are already carving out new roles to address talent shortages. We found that they tend to focus on one of four primary roles, depending on the target audience and strategic objectives. Figure 7.2 depicts the main clusters of corporate universities commonly found.

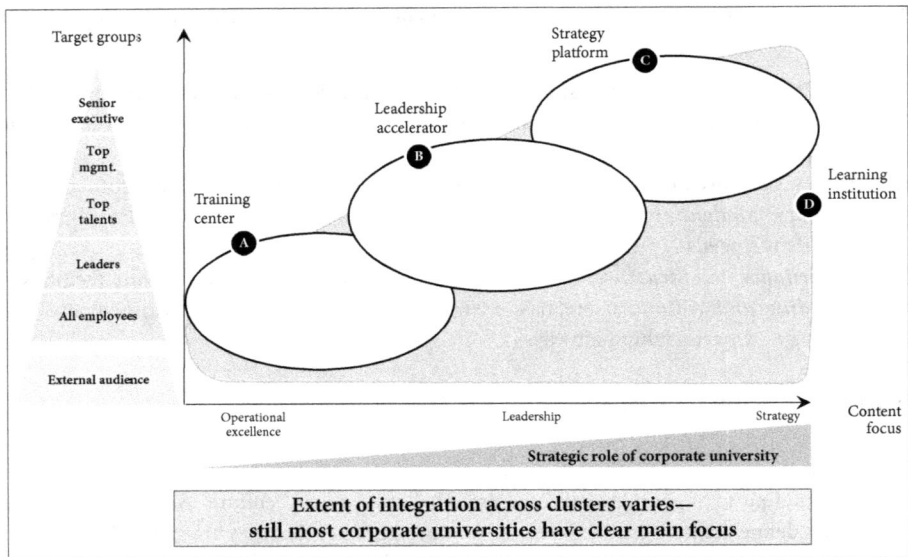

Figure 7.2: Main clusters of corporate universities commonly found

Note: *Corporate-universities assigned to main focus. For some universities an overlap with neighboring functions can be observed*

Source: *Expert interviews; BCG analysis, 2013 by The Boston Consulting Group, Inc.*

According to Figure 7.2, the main clusters of corporate universities are:

- **Training centre.** In this role, the corporate university provides training to regular employees and organisational leaders. The goal is to achieve operational excellence and drive alignment around key organisational processes and standards.
- **Leadership accelerator.** Targeting middle and top management to foster an organisation-wide leadership culture is the focus of this role. By bringing together diverse groups of organisational leaders, these programmes create networks that connect participants long after formal training is completed.
- **Strategy platform.** As organisations strive to improve their strategic capability, corporate universities are becoming catalysts for developing and embedding organisational strategy. These programmes target senior and top management with content directly relevant to the organisation's strategy. The goal is to tie professional development to specific challenges and embed the learning process in strategy development.
- **Learning network.** Creating a learning culture and ongoing learning opportunities beyond the classroom is the charge of these programmes, which target a broad base of management and employees in order to fortify functional, technical, and management skills.

Figure 7.3 gives examples of organisations located within the above discussed clusters.

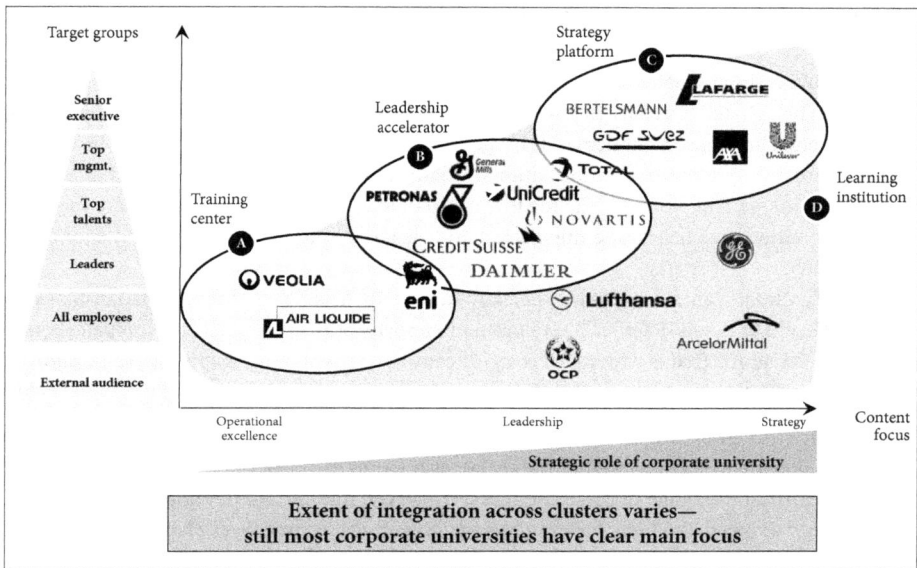

Figure 7.3: Examples of organisations located within the respective clusters
Note: *Corporate-universities assigned to main focus. For some universities an overlap with neighboring functions can be observed*
Source: *Expert interviews; BCG analysis, 2013 by The Boston Consulting Group, Inc.*

Expanding impact

Corporate universities operate in dynamic contexts. They are continually adapting their models to meet the demands of new strategies and new trends such as, for example, digital, acquisitions and market volatility. Corporate universities rarely remain permanently restricted to any of the four primary roles described above. Our study found that they follow two primary paths to increase impact:

- *First and most common path: Broadening the target group.* Many corporate universities began by focusing on small populations, such as senior or top management. However, a large number are expanding their outreach to middle management to create network effects among different management levels. Furthermore, many organisations realise the strategic importance of middle managers, who have not in the past been the focus of professional development.
- *Second path: Changing the business model.* A common approach is to expand beyond delivering training to providing expertise on programme development. In its expanded role, the corporate university acts as an internal consultant for organisational units and regional or local learning departments.

Although not a primary path for expansion, supporting change is another means of increasing impact. Corporate universities can develop specific content and programmes to support organisational change and transformation.

Building Block 3: Target Audience and Content

The curriculum should match the corporate university's objectives, scope, and target audience. It should also be updated to ensure that it is in line with business objectives and needs. In emerging markets, balancing the content demands of different target groups is especially important.

Corporate universities at multinational organisations must tackle a triple challenge in emerging markets. The same is true for the global challengers emerging from these markets. Each must train three levels of employees: senior leaders, middle managers, and employees in general.

"The competition for talent is especially intense in Asia," says Hans-Christian Marxen, head of HR at BASF Asia-Pacific. "Development opportunities are crucial to attract and retain talent in this region. That is why BASF is significantly strengthening its approach and piloting global lifelong learning efforts in Asia."

a. In our 2012 study, we found that in the BRICS countries, only 15% to 30% of *university graduates* are immediately employable. We also found that a *lack of managerial skills* is the most critical challenge in these countries.[8] However, finding and developing talent is only part of the issue. In China, for example, the percentage of employees planning to stay with their current employer is far smaller than in much of the rest of the world: 18.8%, compared with 44.9% in Germany and 38.2% in the U.S. Attrition rates across industries have soared into the double digits.[9]

    Global leadership development is the biggest and longest-standing mandate for multinational organisations. We have observed that adaptive leaders who can recognise, shape, and inspire potential talent are a key differentiator in today's best-run organisations.[10]

    Senior leaders in emerging markets must embody an organisation's values and bring those values to bear in constantly changing multicultural settings. These leaders must also have the flexibility to navigate complex challenges while steering a course in line with the organisation's strategies.

b. The second challenge is middle management. For the most part, organisations have focused their management training on senior executives and high-potential employees. But the need for effective middle managers in emerging markets is ballooning and cannot be met with expatriates. Locals need to be trained and developed. However, the educational systems of these countries do not focus on developing the interpersonal and managerial skills needed to function in large global organisations.

c. Finally, *public education* is falling short in the development of needed functional and vocational skills. In contrast to Western Europe and the United States, vocational training in most emerging markets is rare. In India, for example, only 11.3% of people aged 15 to 29 receive technical or vocational training. As a result, corporate universities are stepping in and developing everything from basic office and team skills to technical expertise.[11]

Most corporate universities focus on leadership or strategy development. Ninety-five percent of the executives we interviewed cited leadership development as the focus of their curricula. Developing a common company culture was important to 70%. Only 33% reported that their corporate university concentrates on content for the broader employee base.

In addition, corporate universities need to segment their audience by career stage. The speed of change in business and its increasing uncertainty call for an adaptive organisation with leaders who can react quickly to new challenges. Corporate universities should provide specific developmental opportunities for middle managers at successive career stages to ensure that, as they move up the ladder, their adaptive-leadership skills keep pace. Age can be another important variable. In developed countries, ageing workers are staying on the job longer and their skills need to meet demand. Corporate universities must provide lifelong learning experiences to ensure that the capabilities of these workers remain fresh.

Building Block 4: Delivery Model

Our interviewees cited three distinct trends in the effort to boost the quality and impact of corporate-university offerings: innovating programme content; leveraging Web 2.0; and developing more robust collaboration strategies. But a general strategic gap exists that can significantly diminish the impact of every one of these efforts.

A strategic shortfall

The training value chain covers the learning spectrum from assessing needs to measuring the impact of offerings, as reflected in Figure 7.4. Yet most corporate universities address only programme development and delivery. Only 14 percent address strategic capability by rigorously analysing workforce demographics, retention levers, and employability issues. Systematic planning is a missing link that is central to relevance and impact.

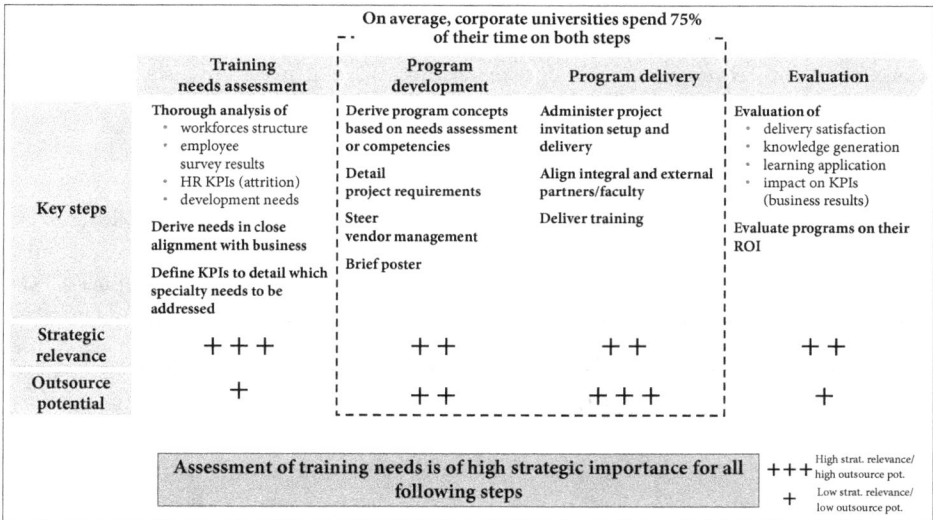

	On average, corporate universities spend 75% of their time on both steps			
	Training needs assessment	**Program development**	**Program delivery**	**Evaluation**
Key steps	Thorough analysis of • workforces structure • employee survey results • HR KPIs (attrition) • development needs Derive needs in close alignment with business Define KPIs to detail which specialty needs to be addressed	Derive program concepts based on needs assessment or competencies Detail project requirements Steer vendor management Brief poster	Administer project invitation setup and delivery Align integral and external partners/faculty Deliver training	Evaluation of • delivery satisfaction • knowledge generation • learning application • impact on KPIs (business results) Evaluate programs on their ROI
Strategic relevance	+ + +	+ +	+ +	+ +
Outsource potential	+	+ +	+ + +	+

Assessment of training needs is of high strategic importance for all following steps	+ + + High strat. relevance/ high outsource pot.
	+ Low strat. relevance/ low outsource pot.

Figure 7.4: Most relevant steps of training value chain not yet addressed by corporate universities
Source: *Expert interviews; BCG analysis, 2013 by The Boston Consulting Group, Inc.*

The strategic shortfall is also evident in the evaluation process. Most respondents (78%) reported that they evaluate participant satisfaction with content, delivery, and facilities. Learning outcomes are assessed exclusively through employee surveys. Only 11% measure the overall impact of their programmes on business outcomes.

Integrating with employee development

For maximum impact, corporate-university offerings should be integrated into the organisation's leadership and employee-development processes. At Unilever, for example, the head of the corporate university is part of the leadership development function and reports to the chief HR officer through the head of leadership development.

Learning innovations and Web 2.0

To create meaningful, company-specific learning experiences, organisations are developing customised case studies that reflect their industry, opportunities, and challenges. The case experience simulates real team-based decision-making processes. Senior managers often serve as coaches. In some cases, participants with specific backgrounds are selected to develop learning experiences for the entire group. Those experiences include interactive role-playing exercises that develop leadership styles. In a similar vein, some corporate universities use actual organisational assignments to ensure that participants internalise the lessons learned and use them in their work.

On the technology front, 24% of the executives we interviewed said that Web 2.0 is a vitally important trend. They expect it to change the face of organisational learning and to ground an organisation's ability to create the ongoing internal and external connections that are the hallmarks of a learning organisation. Although corporate universities are developing e-learning platforms to complement face-to-face programmes, Web 2.0 applications are the focus of technology. Still in the early stages of development, Web 2.0 is seen by many as the technology that will foster ongoing knowledge creation through communities of practice and networks of peers and experts.

Nearly a quarter of respondents said that becoming a learning organisation is a top priority. These organisations want to create dynamic learning processes that overcome the silos among employees, training departments, and organisational leaders. These processes can ensure that an organisation is developing the leaders it needs by fostering strategic thinking and leadership capabilities.

Building Block 5: Governance and Structure

To a large degree, a corporate university's ability to gain companywide acceptance depends on how well it is integrated into the organisational structure. Reporting lines play a significant role. CEO involvement is one of the most critical success factors. In leading organisations CEOs ensure that content is in synch with enterprise and business unit priorities. A close connection to top management demonstrates that the corporate university is a key strategic vehicle. "Close CEO and senior-management involvement is what links the corporate university to the strategy process," says UniCredit's Simioni. "Only through this link can learning leave the classroom and become rooted in real work."

Yet only 32% of respondents said that their corporate university reports to the board and the CEO. Another 37% said it reports directly to the top level of human resources. The remainder said that their corporate university reports to the wider learning and development organisation or to other HR units.

Advisory boards that include internal business leaders can ensure close ties to the organisation. By working closely with the organisation, the advisory board creates a tight link between programmes and organisational strategy. In addition, the board's international makeup helps the organisation to adapt programmes to meet regional requirements.

Accounting for the money

Of the executives we interviewed, only 9% said that their corporate university is fully financed through a standalone budget. To ensure alignment and accountability, most corporate universities charge for some of their services using one of two models: (i) a full-invoicing model (54%) under which nearly all costs are allocated to the business; or (ii) a co-financing model (38%), under which the corporate university assumes the costs of programme development and charges the organisation for delivery.

Structuring options

Over the last decade, globalisation has driven corporate universities away from centralised campuses. The trend now is toward decentralised structures where learning programmes can be regionalised. Figure 7.5 gives examples of different campus setups commonly seen. Local operations also avoid excessive travel costs and underutilised central facilities. In 2000, 45% of corporate universities maintained a major campus or facility. By 2012, the number had dropped to 22%. Some organisations adopt a hybrid model, sharing a major facility with partners and establishing their own regional hubs in key areas.

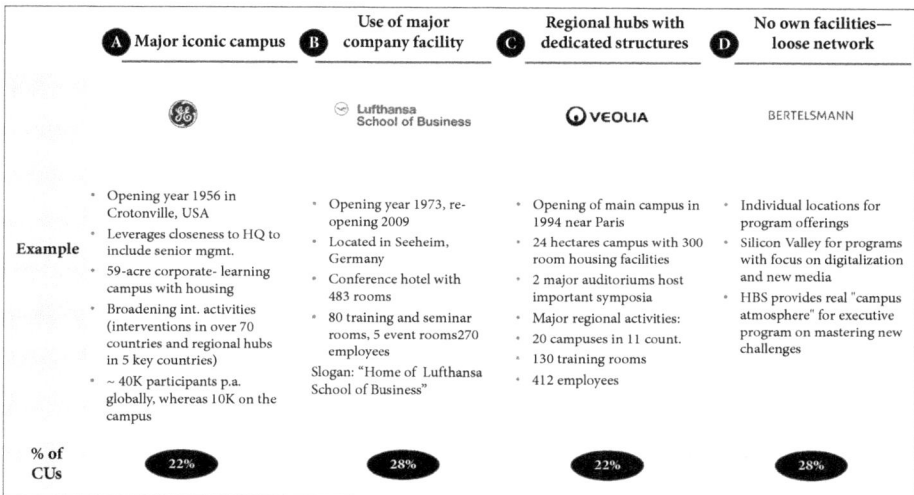

	A Major iconic campus	**B** Use of major company facility	**C** Regional hubs with dedicated structures	**D** No own facilities— loose network
	GE	Lufthansa School of Business	VEOLIA	BERTELSMANN
Example	• Opening year 1956 in Crotonville, USA • Leverages closeness to HQ to include senior mgmt. • 59-acre corporate- learning campus with housing • Broadening int. activities (interventions in over 70 countries and regional hubs in 5 key countries) • ~ 40K participants p.a. globally, whereas 10K on the campus	• Opening year 1973, re-opening 2009 • Located in Seeheim, Germany • Conference hotel with 483 rooms • 80 training and seminar rooms, 5 event rooms 270 employees Slogan: "Home of Lufthansa School of Business"	• Opening of main campus in 1994 near Paris • 24 hectares campus with 300 room housing facilities • 2 major auditoriums host important symposia • Major regional activities: • 20 campuses in 11 count. • 130 training rooms • 412 employees	• Individual locations for program offerings • Silicon Valley for programs with focus on digitalization and new media • HBS provides real "campus atmosphere" for executive program on mastering new challenges
% of CUs	22%	28%	22%	28%

Figure 7.5: Examples of different campus setups commonly seen
Source: *Expert interviews; BCG analysis, 2013 by The Boston Consulting Group, Inc.*

Size and scale matter

Although the size of a corporate university depends on its scope, our research found that the average staffing level is slightly less than 3 FTEs per 10 000 company FTEs.[ii] As a best practice, corporate universities maintain a dedicated staff for administration, direction setting, and curriculum development. A core staff creates a foundation to achieve significant scale effects.

Programme delivery, for example, can be outsourced or covered by other staff serving as internal faculty, allowing the corporate university to scale up or down easily. In economic downturns, the use of third-party facilitators, even developers, can be reduced to meet financial circumstances without cutting core administrative and leadership resources.

Building Block 6: Branding and Alliances

Over the past few years signature leadership programmes with traditional business school offerings have somewhat fallen out of favour. They are perceived by many of the executives we interviewed as too expensive. The emphasis now is on individually designed offerings, blending customised and open enrolment programmes.

---

ii   One FTE (fulltime equivalent) is equivalent to the number of hours worked by one employee on a fulltime basis. FTE calculations are used to convert the number of hours worked by several part-time employees to the number of hours worked by fulltime employees (also referred to as FTEs).

Usually the corporate university will build its own faculty network with specialised expertise. Corporate universities often work directly with a particular professor or with more specialised niche providers in their network. As a result business schools are becoming learning consultants, providing a strong network of specialists and experts to meet an organisation's specific needs.

As corporate universities become increasingly professional, strong internal brands can provide a stamp of approval similar to that of partnerships with major business schools. Moreover, extensive internal marketing can underscore the message that all training and development activities have a common touch and feel, further strengthening the corporate university's link to the company.

Key Success Factors

In addition to the six building blocks described above, seven keys to success in developing a corporate university were cited by nearly all the executives we interviewed.

Engage the CEO

Lacking support from the CEO or the board can result in low organisational acceptance. The corporate university should develop a close relationship with the CEO and enlist him/her to help shape the corporate university's offerings to fit the organisation's strategic imperatives. Individual board members can be drawn into the fold as sponsors of specific programmes.

Connect to the organisation strategy

A tenuous link to the organisation's strategic objectives will put the value of the corporate university in question. To strengthen the link, learning objectives should support the capabilities required by the organisation's strategy. A thorough needs assessment is central to identifying the capability and skills gaps that must be filled to support the corporate strategy. In addition, top-talent-development programmes should prepare participants to forge new strategies.

Stay close to the organisation

If the organisation is not involved in curriculum and programme development, the corporate university risks falling short of expectations. The corporate university should collaborate closely with the organisation in order to understand its needs thoroughly. Representatives from the organisation should sit on corporate-university advisory boards.

Provide high-calibre offerings

If adequate resources are not available, the offerings will not be competitive. The staff of the corporate university should be restructured to include learning experts who can develop high-quality programmes that outperform those of competitors. Organisational representatives should be engaged to translate organisational needs into employee capabilities. The corporate university should also have managers who can oversee complex, global offerings.

Create links with employee development processes

Professional development should include relevant programmes that are required of employees before they take on new assignments or positions. This will give employees the opportunity to use what they have learned on the job.

Measure the value

If performance and impact are not measured, the corporate university's value will not be clear. Corporate universities should identify the capabilities and skills that the organisation needs and measure the impact of learning programmes against those needs. Organisational units should be invoiced at full cost so that they can compare the corporate university's value with that of open enrolment programmes.

Market internally and externally

Offering first-rate programmes that employees are not aware of will defeat much of the corporate university's purpose. The corporate university should enlist top management to advocate for its strategic importance. It should articulate the role that it plays in the employee value proposition. Both internal and external marketing should use branding that is consistent across audiences.

Assessing the Opportunity

Many executives recognise the importance of lifelong learning to meet the talent challenges of the coming decades. As a first step in considering a corporate university or improving existing training and development efforts, we suggest that executives consider the key questions shown below.

Objectives and strategic setup

- What is the primary objective of our efforts, and is there a clearly defined strategic scope and focus in line with overall organisational goals?
- What is the primary target group for our curricula and content, and how are these features linked to our overall objectives?
- How are our training offerings strategically linked to our development processes and decisions?

Curriculum

- How many offerings do we have for each target group, and what are the costs: overall and per employee, business unit, and region?
- How do we link content development and programme evaluation to overall organisational strategy?
- Do we work closely with the organisation to assess its needs?
- How do our offerings prepare employees for future challenges?
- Do we deliver content in a way that ensures a lasting effect on our organisation and employees?

Infrastructure

- Do we have the appropriate infrastructure to deliver our offerings?
- Do we have a clear internal and external branding and marketing strategy?
- Do we have the appropriate costing mechanisms?
- Do we have the right number and type of external partners? Do we collaborate well?
- Do we invest our budget in ways that add value to the company and employees?

Conclusion

Developing powerful HR capabilities is essential for success as needed talent becomes increasingly scarce. Corporate universities can become a strategic platform to develop these capabilities and anchor an organisation's ability to attract, develop, and retain the talent it will need. In turn these capabilities build a virtuous circle. As an organisation's reputation as a people company is boosted by the professional development opportunities that it offers, it can attract the most highly qualified employees and further develop them to meet competitive pressures.

Endnotes

1   World Economic Forum (WEF) and BCG, 2011.
2   PwC, 2008.
3   Strack et al., 2012b.
4   Caye et al., 2012.
5   McAteer & Pino, 2011.
6   Strack et al., 2012a.
7   Boston Consulting Group (BCG), 2011.
8   Caye et al., 2012.
9   Corporate Executive Board (CEB) and BCG, 2011.
10 Torres & Rimmer, 2011, 2012.
11 TeamLease, 2009.

References

Boston Consulting Group (BCG). 2011. 'Corporate universities: An engine for human capital'. *bcg.perspectives*. Boston, MA: Boston Consulting Group (BCG). [Online]. Available: https://www.bcgperspectives. com/content/articles/human_resources_leadership_talent_corporate_universities_engine_human_ capital/. [Accessed 6 August 2016].

Caye, J-M, Bhalla, V, Aguiar, M & Nettesheim, C. 2012. 'When growth outstrips talent: Five strategies for emerging markets'. *bcg.perspectives*, April. [Online]. Available: https://www.bcgperspectives.com/ content/articles/globalization_people_management_human_resources_when_growth_outstrips_ talent/. [Accessed 6 August 2016].

Corporate Executive Board (CEB). 2011. '*Engagement trends: Q3 2011. Discretionary effort and intent to stay by geography, function and industry*'. bcgperspectives, October. Arlington County, VA: Corporate Executive Board (CEB). [Online]. Available: https://www.bcgperspectives.com/content/articles/ human_resources_leadership_talent_corporate_universities_engine_human_capital/. [Accessed 6 August 2016].

McAteer, P & Pino, M. 2011. 'The business case for creating a corporate university'. *Corporate University Xchange*, 12 September.

PwC. 2008. *Managing tomorrow's people: Millennials at work—perspectives from a new generation*. [Online]. Available: https://www.pwc.de/de/prozessoptimierung/assets/managing_tomorrows_people_ millennials_at_work-perspectives_from_a_new_generation.pdf. [Accessed 6 August 2016].

Strack, R, Caye, J-M, von der Linden, C, Quirós, H & Haen, P. 2012a. 'Realizing the value of people management: From capability to profitability. BCG and World Federation of People Management Associations report'. *bcg.perspectives*, July. [Online]. Available: https://www.bcgperspectives.com/content/articles/people_management_human_resources_leadership_from_capability_to_profitability/. [Accessed 6 August 2016].

Strack, R, Caye, J-M, Bhalla, V, Tollman, P, von der Linden, C, Haen, P, et al. 2012b. 'Creating people advantage 2012: Mastering HR challenges in a two-speed world. BCG and World Federation of People Management Associations report'. *bcg.perspectives*, October. [Online]. Available: https://www.bcgperspectives.com/content/articles/people_management_human_resources_leadership_creating_people_advantage_2012/. [Accessed 6 August 2016].

TeamLease. 2009. *India labour report, 2009: The geographic mismatch & a ranking of Indian states by their labour ecosystem*. [Online]. Available: http://www.teamlease.com/media/1149/teamlease_labourreport2009.pdf. [Accessed 6 August 2016].

Torres, R & Rimmer, N. 2011. 'The five traits of highly adaptive leadership teams: What senior leaders do differently'. *bcg.perspectives*, December. [Online]. Available: https://www.bcgperspectives.com/content/articles/leadership_organization_design_five_traits_of_highly_adaptive_leadership_teams/. [Accessed 6 August 2016].

Torres, R & Rimmer, N. 2012. 'Winning practices of adaptive leadership teams. BCG report'. *bcg.perspectives*, April. [Online]. Available: https://www.bcgperspectives.com/content/articles/leadership_people_management_human_resources_winning_practices_of_adaptive_leadership_teams/. [Accessed 6 August 2016].

World Economic Forum (WEF) and BCG. 2011. *Global talent risk – seven responses*. Cologny/Geneva, Switzerland, CHE: World Economic Forum (WEF) in collaboration with Boston Consulting Group (BCG). [Online]. Available: http://www.workinfo.com/Articles/global_talent2011.htm. [Accessed 6 August 2016].

SECTION 5

LEADERSHIP STORIES

Chapter 9

LEADERSHIP STORIES

Introduction

In its very essence, the organisation is a dialogical network of interpersonal interconnections based on conversations, expressed in the form of stories. Stories are naturally-occurring phenomena in organisations through which information, shared experiences, expectations, culture, and identity are passed on. Stories are the very fabric of organisational life. They add a psychological dimension to organisational life through its feeling and experiencing dimension in the form of sense-making, meaning-giving, as well as emotional attachment and involvement which rational, empirical information and lack of knowledge cannot provide.

Storytelling infuses the whole Strategic Leadership Value Chain. It is persuasive leadership-in-action. A story as a form of conversation is capable of representing and transferring complex, multidimensional organisational realities to listeners in a simple and effortless way in order to make sense of, and give meaning and purpose to, organisational reality.

At its most basic level, storytelling as a conversation (or dialogue) refers to what is being said and listened to between people. The word 'dialogue' stems from two Greek roots, "*dia*" and "*logos*", jointly suggesting the sense of "meaning flowing through". Stories help organisational members to make sense of who they are, where they come from and fit in, and what they want to be. They help reduce organisational uncertainty, complexity and ambiguity by quickly and coherently disseminating information; they frame organisational events through their value-laden features; and they promote organisational culture and identification by establishing a context for organisational members.

Using stories is one of the best ways to:

- make abstract concepts meaningful;
- help connect people and ideas;
- inspire imagination and motivate action;
- give "breathing space" in the frenetic and merciless task-driven nature of the organisation;
- allow different perspectives to emerge;
- create sense, coherence, and meaning;
- develop value-centric descriptions of situations, allowing knowledge to be applied and solutions to be found;
- convey organisational values and culture;
- communicate complex messages simply;
- connect people into a shared frame of reference; and
- inspire change.

In the *first instance* leaders are, and have to be, storytellers about themselves: from where they have come; who they are; what they stand for; what they believe in; what they want to achieve and how; and what they want to leave behind as a legacy. The character, competence, connectedness, caring and commitment of leaders are manifested *inter alia* in how well they understand, and are able and willing to share, their personal journeys as leaders: from the past, through the present, into the future. It is a most powerful way in which to connect with others.

In the *second instance*, leaders have to be able to tell the story of the organisation they are currently involved in: the identity and ideology of the organisation; where the organisation has come from; its desired future destination and legacy; the journey travelled to date by the organisation; the journey still to be travelled; and how things are done and not done in the organisation.

This Section provides examples of the first kind of leadership stories: leaders' stories about themselves as leaders.

The accompanying box gives a list of the leaders whose stories follow – with their respective core themes – are included in this Section.

LEADER'S STORY	THEME OF STORY
Cheryl Carolus	*Leaders must lead by example*
Johan van Zyl	*Get to know yourself early on in your career*
Ali Bacher	*Captaining on and off the field*
Ian Donald	*Being an authentic and confident leader*
Herman Mashaba	*Good leaders are guided by reality, not wishful thinking*
Pfungwa Serima	*Head in the Clouds and feet on the ground*

References

Boje, D. 2008. *Storytelling organizations.* Thousand Oaks, CA: Sage.

Boyce, M.E. 1996. 'Organisational story and storytelling: A critical review' *Journal of Organisational Change Management*, 9(5):5-26.

Christie, P. 2009. *Every leader a story teller – storytelling skills for personal leadership.* Johannesburg, ZA: Knowres.

Denning, S. 2011. *The leader's guide to storytelling*, San Francisco, CA: Jossey-Bass

Gabriel, Y. 2000). *Storytelling in organisations: Facts, fictions and fantasies.* New York, NY: Oxford University Press.

Ibarra, H & Lineback, K. 2005. 'What's your story?' *Harvard Business Review*, 1–7, January.

Veldsman, D & May, M. S. 2012. 'The stories that leaders tell during organisational change: The search for meaning during organisational transformation'. Unpublished Masters thesis, University of South Africa, Pretoria, South Africa.

Leaders Must Lead by Example

Cheryl Carolus

Article published in Sake Beeld on 26 November 2015.
Translated from Afrikaans. Used with permission

Leadership is a rare privilege – by definition, only a few can lead the many – and a wonderful opportunity to shape the future you desire. Needless to say, this comes with a huge burden of responsibility which calls for wisdom, but holds the threat of incarceration if you exercise this duty in an irresponsible manner.

The world is in a sorry state. Economies are under pressure, and previously rare events which have now become commonplace, like suicide bombings, increasingly define our understanding of what it means to be safe. Conflict has become an intra-national phenomenon with international consequences. The issues which cause conflict today are markedly different from those which once unleashed two world wars.

Our understanding of power has changed. Nowadays, those in power are more interested in 'controlling' than 'ruling' the masses. Governments are but one link in the chain of governance which ensures that societies function optimally.

A great deal of time and serious introspection is needed before we can develop social theories which fully encompass and institutionalise this knowledge. So great is the need, South Africa is compelled to adopt a 'fast forward' mode in everything it does. Here, the opportunities and the risks are much greater than one would find in a boring, run-of-the-mill democracy.

In this value chain, elected leaders play a vital role. They must strike a balance where conflicting needs arise, while serving the interests of the majority. I was furious, to say the least, that our elected leaders wasted so much time on ridiculous semantics as regards the private residence of an empowered citizen (the president) and the dress code of those in power who like a touch of 'bling'. I am livid that our parliament allowed the president to be subjected to political mud-slinging and uncouth behaviour. In my view, that is not leadership.

Even more lamentable are the actions of the various party leaders that overshadow the unbelievable achievements of many in those institutions. Achievements which even more established democracies cannot lay claim to, such as the wide-spread roll-out of antiretroviral medication; women in public leadership positions; the inclusion of people with disabilities; scientific innovations such as the Square Kilometre Array project; and world-renowned achievements in the arts.

Time is running out – we have to defuse the ticking time bombs of inequality and poverty. We cannot waste another 20 per cent of a democratic term in office. What will cure these ailments? Inclusivity and accountability.

The benefits of women's participation are evident on a global scale. We would be extremely short-sighted not to utilise our capabilities. Worldwide, women now make up more than 50 per cent of all graduates. The same goes for people with disabilities, who are fully capable of helping us tackle these significant challenges. To those whom history has marginalised, I say: Our constitution is a gift, if you choose to use it. Going it alone is one option, but working with others in an organised way is better. That way you can help to build a strong society. This not only applies to the public sector – truth be told, when it comes to inclusivity, the private sector is lagging behind.

How many of us use the mechanisms which are in place to ensure accountability, also as regards promulgating laws in this country? Do you participate in public hearings at provincial or national government level? Or in sectoral committee meetings? Do you serve on a school governing body? Those who wish to hamper progress in this country frequently make use of these mechanisms.

As a country, we can do so much better. We must compel our leaders to do a better job – in both the private and the public sector, as well as in the political arena. Accountability is plagued by two issues: corruption and the fact that the lives of the poor seemingly do not matter. Perhaps the time has come to consider mobilising public opinion as well as resources to prosecute any leader who benefits from corruption in the private or public sector. Perhaps we should use the full might of the law to prosecute an executive director if an employee is killed in the workplace. It may be time to launch a more thorough investigation into the impact of certain non-governmental organisations (NGOs), while simultaneously aligning their salaries with those of their counterparts in the private sector.

Let those of us who bear the title of leader, lead the way by example.

Cheryl Carolus is the Executive Chairperson of the investment management firm, Peotona, and non-Executive Chairperson of the mining company, Gold Fields. She is a former Executive Head of SA Tourism and also served as South African High Commissioner in London. Until 2012, she was the Chairperson of South African Airways.

Get To Know Yourself as a Leader
Early On in Your Career

Johan van Zyl

Article published in Sake Beeld on 18 June 2015.
Translated from Afrikaans. Used with permission

In life many opportunities present themselves, but very few of us grasp them enthusiastically and meaningfully, with both hands. In my view this is the first important step towards true leadership: the ability to identify and act on opportunities. Arguably, one of the main indicators of weak leadership is an inability to identify actual strategic issues, which then culminates in missed opportunities. An organisation which lets an important window of opportunity close, is already on a slippery slope towards obsolescence.

Clearly, to be successful within a given context, you need to focus on those aspects which will strengthen your unique leadership style. Personally, I cannot but overemphasise the importance of focus. Slacking off is never an option – and in my view, a healthy dose of impatience is a prerequisite. My advice is to determine where you can make a difference, and then to focus on measurable outcomes, because measurables influence behaviour. A leader not only needs to recognise and reward achievement, but also to penalise underachievement.

I advocate an eclectic management style – a mixed bag, if you will. Many would categorise themselves as a specific type of leader. In my view a specific situation calls for a specific type of leadership. In some cases it is best to take control and say: 'This is how we're going to do it.' In other instances it is better to take a step back. Easier said than done, especially when things are not going according to plan.

South Africa faces a number of core challenges: widespread poverty, relatively high unemployment, an oversupply of lowly or unschooled labour. All these factors conspire to limit our economic growth to a snail's pace. Leaders in the private sector in this country cannot solely prioritise business. It is imperative for organisations to make social and socio-economic issues part of their strategic plan, along with a corporate social responsibility programme as part of their daily business dealings. I do not advocate that heads of companies dabble in politics. Rather, they should investigate how a changing socio-economic landscape will impact business confidence in their specific industry or sector.

Business people face two other important challenges: workplace diversity and black economic empowerment. Despite being seen as challenges, these issues provide wonderful business opportunities. A more diverse workforce – especially at senior levels – implies that more diverse ideas will be forthcoming, which will make the company more resilient within an already complex business environment. A diversity of ideas is the life blood of successful innovation.

One aspect of leadership which benefits from more inclusive discourse is values. If leadership revolves around taking responsibility for the bigger picture, rather than being all about power, we create space for conversations around common values. Companies should follow a top-down approach. This means that the leader sets the pace and the personnel follow his/her example.

As a leader, where does personal development fit into the equation? I argue that this is vital in the early stages of an individual's career, and something for which each of us must accept personal responsibility. It is imperative not only to know yourself, but to be honest with yourself: about both your strengths and your weaknesses.

In conclusion, I believe true leadership reflects the power and success of a team, rather than the abilities of a single individual.

From 2003 to June 2015, Dr Johan van Zyl served as Executive Group Head of Sanlam. He is the former head of Santam, and served as Vice Chancellor of the University of Pretoria and as a consultant for the World Bank. He holds two PhDs, one of which is a DSc in agriculture. He currently serves on the board of numerous companies and is a member of the Royal Society of South Africa.

Captaining On and Off the Field

Ali Bacher

Interview conducted by Wilhelm Crous of Knowledge Resources during April 2016.

Leading on the field

In my book top leaders and captains of sports teams have a lot in common. They are born with the gene to motivate people. I do not believe this is a skill that can be taught. I have worked with magnificent cricketers such as Jacques Kallis, one of South Africa's greatest all-rounders, who never wanted to be a captain, a leader. It just was not part of who he was. Whereas Hansie Cronje was someone who I considered a born leader throughout his entire career. He had the ability to motivate and stimulate a team.

It was the same for me. I was always able to captain teams. From primary school, where I captained soccer, cricket and tennis teams right through to captaining South Africa's Under 21s and then the Springboks. I really enjoyed every moment, doing my best to motivate players to improve their performances. That is what real leadership is about.

Whenever a cricket team is selected, there are probably about nine guys who are guaranteed places. They are doing well and you do not have to worry about them. But at every level there are always two or three who are a bit nervous. They might have had a few bad games and are feeling the pressure that if they fail again they could be dropped from the team. Those were the guys I used to focus on, without them being overtly aware of it. I would be there encouraging them at net practices and on the field, subtly lifting their performance. I not only enjoyed doing this, but I really wanted to do it.

It is all about the strategy

Being a captain also meant working out strategies which I loved doing. I would call a player or two before a game, trying to get their input or lift their performance, whatever it took.

I particularly remember one of the most extraordinary games I ever played in. I was captaining our school team and we were playing another school, our big local rival in a two-day game over a Wednesday and a Saturday. The Saturday game was a disaster for us as we found ourselves 29, all out and we had to follow on. Their captain came up to me after the game and said, 'perhaps we should call it a day and forget about next Wednesday?' I said absolutely not. It's part of the programme and you must arrive on Wednesday. The following Monday I rounded up a couple of my teammates and we went to the back of the science laboratory where we put together a strategy on how to beat these guys. I was always strategising. Wednesday arrived. They showed up 22 minutes late. By 4 pm I had worked out we needed about 170 runs to put us in a good position to win. I declared leaving them 105 minutes to get 70 runs. We bowled them out …

A born leader

There was a famous English captain, Mike Brearley (1977-1980) who although his test batting average was only about 24 – poor for a recognised test batsman – successfully captained England 31 times out of 39 matches. He was known as a great leader. He had the ability to bring out the best in his players, such as Ian Botham, who eventually took over the captaincy from him. When he finished his test career he became a psychologist, which was a perfect transition for him. Again a born leader.

Leading through people

You also have those captains who lead from the front by example, such as Eddie Barlow and AB de Villiers. Eddie Barlow was always up there at the front, getting runs, taking wickets – that was part of his personality. I was not like that. I was more of a quiet behind-the-scenes kind of guy – trying to get the best out of people by my own methods. I led through people. Leading through people is perhaps more sustainable. Morné du Plessis was a great example of leading through people.

Pressing the right buttons

Motivating people is not one size fits all. Take a player such as Graeme Pollock. There was a player you had to constantly assure he was the greatest batsman the world had ever seen. He liked hearing that. It motivated him and made him feel good about himself.

When I was captain of Transvaal, now the Highveld Lions, I had a fantastic medium fast bowler, Don Mackay-Coghill, who remains my best friend and now lives in Perth, Australia. We had a very ordinary attack in that team but he was our kingpin. I had to make sure I got the best out of him. There was only one way and that was to make him really angry. What I did was to get other players to subtly say to him: "You know what Barlow said about you the other day…" and he used to fall for it. He would get provoked, a bit cross, and he would go firing away. It was all about pressing the right buttons.

Before a match I would quietly phone some members of my team enquiring how they were feeling, how things were going: "Could I help?" This gave me a great insight as to their mindset before a game.

Although AB de Villiers leads from the front, he also falls into the category of a great leader. He is a very special person. In all my interactions with him I have come to know him as one of the most sincere, down to earth players I have ever dealt with. People like this and others, such as Morné du Plessis and Francois Pienaar, are meant to be leaders. People and players look up to them and respect them.

Great leaders on the field

There is far more to being a great leader than just ball skills. Mark Taylor, captain of Australia from 1994 to 1999 was not only a great tactical player and captain, but had a very warm disposition. A great mix for a captain. And then there is Steve Waugh, who took over the captaincy from Taylor in 1999, whose cricket thinking was unique. There is no other cricketer who has thought more about the game than him. He would look closely at his opposition and then work on how to get them out. He would know which batsman would work best against a particular left arm swing bowler or which bowler would lose their cool if you went after them quickly. This is what goes into making a great captain and leader: great thought processes.

Keeping up the motivation

This is sometimes the hardest part of being a leader. When we played Australia in the 1970 series there were some really brilliant performances. My problem was even though we were winning and giving the Aussies a thumping, how could we keep playing at the same level?

The Aussies had given us a battering in 1935 with the great Donald Bradman and again when they visited in 1949. We should have beaten them in the 1957/58 tour but again they won the series hands down. When they were coming here for the 1969/70 tour we were a young team, but we knew we were good and were very excited to be playing test cricket. We had players such as Barry Richards, Graeme Pollock and Mike Procter. I called them together and said to the team that they knew we had got pummelled by these guys in the past so we must make sure we give them a hiding like they have never had before. At the back of my mind was to try and get some comfort for those guys who had been so horribly beaten in all those previous tests.

We did just that, and if there had been a fifth test match we would have done the same again. South Africa won the series 4-1. We really went after them quietly. We did not shout the odds. It was not just because we had a great team. Sometimes you can have great players and something can go wrong and the aggro can start. There have been great teams with great players who should have won and they did not.

The challenges today

Today's teams face very different challenges. Mainly because of the huge press corps that goes wherever they go these days on and often off the pitch. When I think back for instance to our tour of England in 1965 we had the inimitable Charles Fortune, Gerhard Viviers (Spiekeries), a reporter from SAPA (South African Press Association) and George Scott from the Argus Group. That was it. This meant when we misbehaved – and we did – no one would know about it.

In today's world with social media and mobile phones, pressures on the captain and coach are far more formidable. Wherever you have countries with diversity you will be faced by political correctness. And being a sports leader, a captain, chairman of a union or a coach in these circumstances can be difficult.

My first piece of advice here is learn how to handle the media. I always had good interaction with the media, especially when I was in the administrative side of cricket. I used the media to promote the game. If I had a good idea of something new I thought would promote cricket I would give it to the media. They did not have to call me. Sometimes I would call them at 7am with a story because I knew it was newsworthy and they would publish it. I was proactive. Today very few people in cricket or even other sports know how to handle the media.

From the field to the boardroom, and making risky decisions

In 1981 I became the first CEO of SA Cricket until I left in 2003 after 23 years at the helm. And when I think back to some of the major decisions I made in the eighties I shudder. I remember going for early morning walks and saying out loud to myself: "Are you mad? If this goes south, you're gone!" Fortunately it did not happen.

Today working alongside CEOs making the same mistakes I did, I jump in and quickly tell them that before they make a move, to get approval from the financial guys. Do not wait until the Board meeting and spring your idea on them. Rather go and see the chairman and get him on your side first. I learnt you have to cover yourself. You cannot make huge decisions on your own. Be more democratic, participative in reaching decisions.

Compassion and kindness play a role

There have been many times when I have stepped in outside of my mandate as captain or CEO to help someone out. With Makhaya Ntini in particular, when I heard he had been accused of rape I really found it hard to believe. I went to Advocate Jeremy Gauntlett and asked him to step in and act for Makhaya. Gauntlett told me if he had believed he was guilty he would never have taken the case. He was convicted but it went to appeal, which eventually saw the case thrown out. A great relief.

Transformation in the future – it is all about opportunities

Right now cricket and rugby in South Africa are still producing good players. We have around 30 high schools renowned for continually producing Springbok rugby players alone. These are schools with a culture of these games. They have good coaches, players, headmasters, support staff and parents who attend the games. Grey College is a great example. The question that is being asked is how do we reach young black players. Do we go into the townships? Yes, to initially get their interest in the sports. But will we get players directly from there? No. Unless an African schoolboy has Brian Lara's genes he is not going to make it to a national side without resources, a great coach and support.

All our top young black players today have gone to the right schools. Take the current Proteas: Kagiso Rabada, the dynamic young bowler went to St Stithians; batsman Temba Bavuma to St Davids; Hashim Amla Durban Boys High and Makhaya Ntini, who we sent to Dale College. It is only by spotting talent and then directing them to these kinds of schools that we will get top black players right now. It is just a fact. Even if you are a young white rugby player at an obscure school in a small town. Unless you go to Affies, your chances of becoming a Springbok are small.

Makhaya Ntini is a perfect example of the current status of black players in South Africa. He was spotted by a black coach at the age of 14 at a mini-cricket clinic in a rural area of the Eastern Cape. He had one look at him and contacted one of our top coaches. If Makhaya had not gone to Dale College on a bursary he would still be there: in the townships. Cricket can change lives. We need sporting leaders to make this happen.

Rubbing shoulders with the mighty – what rubbed off

Perhaps the highlight of my career and the greatest lessons in leadership I have gained have come through having the privilege of interacting with people such as Nelson Mandela. The first thing that struck me when I met him was here was this man, imprisoned for 27 years, who has absolutely no malice.

In 1995 when we were hosting the Rugby World Cup he went public on a Friday morning with the decision that he would back the use of the Springbok emblem. The ANC were furious. The next thing I knew an SABC news team were at my door wanting to interview me on whether the same would now apply to cricket. I said we have great respect for President Mandela but we are not going that route. The Springbok emblem for South African cricket represented a period of our history where only whites could play. For us until today the Protea emblem is not a big thing.

A gesture of greatness

The next morning I received a call from President Mandela at 9am. He told me he had watched my interview. He then went on to invite me to have lunch the following Monday. I took two of my Board members and went along to the Union Buildings. It was the day before his birthday. Even though he did not drink, he insisted on opening a bottle of wine to celebrate with lunch. Then he took us outside and went on to explain why he supported the Springbok emblem. He said he knew how important rugby and the Springbok emblem were to the Afrikaner. His decision was because he wanted to thank them for supporting him as the first black president.

The late Steve Tshwete, who went on to become my great friend and colleague, told that he had also received a phone call from the President that day to tell him to bring a number six jersey to Ellis Park. When he asked why, he was firmly told that it did not matter. Just to bring it. Some of the players then told me the rest of the story. At around half past two that day there was a knock on the change room door and the security guard announced that President Mandela is here and would they mind if he came in. He walked in wearing the number six jersey, and went around the room speaking quietly to each player. As Kobus Wiese later said: "There was no way we weren't going to win for him." And how do you describe the reaction when Mandela walked on to the field? That is a leader that comes along once in a century.

Just a word from Madiba

In 1998 the great West Indies cricketers were due to tour South Africa for the first time. Unfortunately they were having an issue with their Board and had holed up in a hotel in London refusing to budge. Another great South African, Jakes Gerwel, who loved cricket passionately and who was Madiba's right-hand man came to the rescue. I told him that I had to go to England to try and persuade these guys to come and play here. He called me back half an hour later. That night I left South Africa with a letter from Madiba in my back pocket. I waited in London until a journalist tipped me off that the West Indies players were coming out of their room to talk to the media. I rushed over and pulled out the letter: my trump card. Brian Lara later told me they then had a meeting, which lasted a whole two minutes before they agreed to come. That was the power of Mandela.

Getting through the tough times

One of the hardest years of my cricketing career had to be England's 1990 rebel cricket tour to South Africa led by Mike Gatting. As soon as word got out they had arrived we started to hear there was going to be trouble. People were angry. We heard rumours that pitches would be invaded, and worse. Once we arrived in Kimberley we saw these were not empty threats. This was reinforced in Pietermaritzburg where I thought Gatting was going to get killed. So I called our Board together and said we have to call it a day. We will have to negotiate a way out. We cannot go on.

From then on I did not hear another word from a single member of my Board. I felt very much on my own. I found out later that Thabo Mbeki, operating from England at the time, was behind much of the protest action. He then got someone to call Michael Katz, the lawyer, to come and see me. He presented me with a mandate with a couple of options. This saw me negotiating with Krish Mackerdhuj – president of the SA Cricket Board at the time – at Michael Katz's house at 2am on how to go on or get out.

We had played quite well in the first part of the tour. There was supposed to be a second leg but I knew it would be crazy to believe this could happen. The SA Cricket Union guys were after me. Ironically the cricket fans in the township were also after me, but for different reasons. They were so angry I was not allowed back in the townships where we had a flourishing cricket programme going.

Fall out and the way forward

Everyone was angry at me. For the first and only time in my life I found myself leaving work at lunchtime, going home, pulling out the telephone plug and refusing to take any calls. I was absolutely finished. It was only after speaking to Van Zyl Slabbert that I saw some light.

A few years previously he had arranged for me to see Aziz Pahad in London about the situation in South African cricket. This time once again he came to my rescue organising a meeting with the late Steve Tshwete. This was a turning point. From then on Tshwete never stopped helping me. He was so credible amongst the African community and the Black Sports Congress. They knew he was backing me and they said fine. Day by day people who had been my adversaries became my best friends. It just took two allies, namely Van Zyl Slabbert and Steve Tshwete to save me.

Krish Mackurdhuj, who was quite a political animal at the time, said to me that he knew what I had been through but that the tour had to take place because it was a game changer for South African sport. It showed that you could not have sporting bodies come to this country without the majority of people's support.

The turning point

The only reason we were able to return to world cricket in 1991 was because we had the support of the ANC. Thabo Mbeki gave me a letter to go to the black cricketing countries, sending Steve with me to get support for our readmission. This was amazing when you think there was no guarantee that there was going to be a democracy. Or, that the ANC would ever really be in power. But they believed in our programme. And that we were genuinely trying to redress imbalances, giving young black cricketers real opportunities.

This came back to bite us badly when in 1999 with Steve Tshwete at my side, I went to The Wanderers for a test match against the West Indies, where South Africa fielded an entirely white team. This was the only time ever during my time as CEO of SA Cricket when I was forced to step in and ask questions. Even though we had Makhaya Ntini in the squad, I had been told although he was coming along well he was off form. At the time I came out publicly to oppose this policy and say that we must never field an all-white team again. This nearly cost me my lifetime friendship with Peter Pollock, the convenor of selectors, as well as making things very difficult between Hansie Cronje and I.

Tough decisions are not always popular

A week later we had a Board meeting. A policy was put in place that in future there would always be a team of colour. The first casualty of this was my nephew – Adam Bacher – whose place was taken by Herschel Gibbs. For the remainder of the tour – the seven, one day matches – we enlarged the squad from 14 to 17 players, adding three promising young black players. I knew the ANC were putting pressure on Steve Tshwete who had himself on the line for South African cricket since the early nineties. It was time for change. Even if some people were angry.

I had always said if you have a CEO of a company and everybody loves him, he has not done his job. Sometimes you have to make tough decisions and knock a few people off the road.

Let life's lessons guide you

Being a good captain and a leader means drawing on experience and the same goes in sport. I was captain of Transvaal at 21 but by the time I was made captain of South Africa I was 28 with seven years of hard cricket behind me. When Graeme Smith was made captain at just 22 I felt that was much too early. It is a huge responsibility to put on such young shoulders and there is no substitute for experience.

In summary

I believe the key features of a great sports leader are: (i) you have to be a natural (born) leader. You must want it and enjoy the pressures of leading; (ii) lead every player differently according to their specific unique strengths and weaknesses; (iii) strategise and pay attention to detail; (iv) prepare for the challenges of leading, i.e. have good communication and media skills; (v) be accessible to the media and supporters; (vi) where applicable, be inclusive and democratic in your decision making; (vii) be proactive; (viii) confront difficult situations. Bring in additional expertise and value advice; (ix) take calculated risks; (x) stay humble; and (xi) lead through others!

Aron Bacher, given the nickname 'Ali' at the age of seven after Ali Baba, studied medicine and practised as a GP for a couple of years. He played in 12 Tests for South Africa, and took over the national captaincy in 1969-70, inheriting what was probably South African cricket's greatest side of all times, including Barry Richards, Mike Procter, Eddie Barlow and a pair of Pollocks. He became MD of the SA Cricket Union in the late 1980s. Seeing the democratic change in SA in the offing, he reinvented himself as South Africa's cricket supremo when the previously separate black and white associations combined to set up the United Cricket Board which he headed until the early 2000s.

Being an Authentic and Confident Leader

Ian Donald

Interviewed on 30 October 2014 by Adriaan Groenewald of
Leadership Platform. Used with permission

Every now and then I meet a leader that comes across as truly authentic with a healthy confidence. Ian Donald, the newly appointed CEO of Nestle SA is such a leader. He has lead in Philippines, Nestle Ice Cream SA, Pakistan together with war-torn Afghanistan and East Africa that includes 21 countries. And now he is back in South Africa to create movement in his motherland.

Authentic and confident leaders have a track record of having created successful movement over and over. Donald has done this in several diverse geographical locations, which is part of why he projects confidence. In fact because of this track record, his reputation and respect for him precedes him. Confidence is "trusting processes that work", and this is the same for leadership. To be a confident leader one must learn to trust leadership processes that work, which presupposes doing it over and over.

The mere announcement that Donald is coming to a country, division or branch triggers movement, action and people anticipating what he wants or expects of them. This is a powerful position to be in, which is part and parcel of an authentic and confident leader. Unfortunately in a world of "immediacy" where leaders want career progression now, and where movement from one position to the next happens fast, together with overall societal change that happens at break-neck pace, these kinds of leaders may become rarer.

Authentic and confident leaders possess the courage to make themselves vulnerable, probably because they have learnt to manage or destruct their ego. They really believe that they are still learning. They admit when they do not know something or when they have made a mistake. While it may not be easy, they accept when others point to their incongruent behaviour; and they are comfortable with engaging staff on all levels. If leaders would only check their egos at the door, the world would be a better place.

Donald says: "I'm now sixty-three but still believe in this principle of learning all the time. I am conscious of what I learn. So going to Pakistan for example, I hope I made a contribution, but boy did I learn, and did I grow as an individual." And he adds: "I find the biggest journey I have been on all my life is knowing myself. And that's still the journey I am on most." This attitude manifests in his everyday behaviour, like walking around, wanting to connect with the people.

Authentic and confident leaders buy into the truth that human beings are driven by deep-rooted values. So they fanatically drive values inside their business, while striving to remain true to their own. They work with the big picture of matching individual needs and values with the organisations, and even broader society. As Donald comments: "It comes back to values all the time – the importance of respect, and the importance of understanding other people, other cultures." He has had to apologise because a staff member challenged his behaviour as being incongruent with values.

Authentic and confident leaders achieve greatness because they usually care relatively little about what others think of them. They are driven by what is right, rather than by how others perceive them. They do not act for approval but for successful movement as leader as required by a particular situation. Because of a tamed ego they do not just change things around them for the sake of changing. They move in, listen, and do what needs to be done. If the situation requires radical change, they do it. If the situation requires them to merely build on what has been achieved, they make this happen as well.

When Donald moved into Pakistan he did not just change everything. At the time he commented: "The correct approach in a business that did not require turnaround but merely wasn't living up to its full potential was not to change everything. In fact, coming in and changing everything, especially as an expat, sends out a clear message that what was done up until then was not respected." He was conscious of showing appreciation for the past and building on it.

Authentic and confident leaders understand that all of the above and more are important, but none of it matters if the business is not profitable and sustainable. "You can't get away from the fact that at the base of it all is to create a sustainable, long-term, growing, profitable business. Otherwise you can't do anything; it all falls apart," explains Donald.

At Nestle they speak of "shared value rather than social responsibility". They feel that to survive in a long-term sustainable way they have to add value all the way through the value chain from beginning to end: from the farmer that provides raw material to the end consumer. Everyone in the value chain must be successful. And then follows the responsibility to add value to broader societal issues like gas emissions, water pollution and so on, which Nestle is very involved with.

The future changes every day. There is so much happening around one that is unexpected and beyond your control. So one has to be prepared to adapt. According to Donald: "Watching the scenery and keeping yourself aware is very critical." For example, the Ebola outbreak is already impacting their business on cocoa supplies for chocolate. "You have got to be aware and cannot be fixed in a vision and direction blindly," says Donald. And so, an authentic and confident leader is very aware of the big picture and uses this to create meaning, purpose.

Ian Donald, the newly appointed CEO of Nestle SA. He has led Nestle Organisations across many countries, mostly in emerging economies.

Good Leaders Arae Guided by Reality, Not Wishful Thinking

Herman Mashaba

*Article published in Sake Beeld on 7 July 2015, translated from Afrikaans,
in combination with an interview during April 2012 conducted by Adriaan
Groenewald of the Leadership Platform. Used with permission*

In South Africa today, we have to focus on political leadership because that is the area where decisions are being taken that are impacting most negatively on the country. We read daily about decisions that appear to be purposely designed to cause harm instead of improve economic conditions for our people. A reality check should be telling the government that decisions they are taking are causing harm. They need to change direction but that is not what is happening. They seem to be determined to keep going in the wrong direction. There are all sorts of international comparisons that can help in making the right decisions to improve South Africa's economic growth but our policy makers seem to be determined to do the opposite of what works in the rest of the world.

You would think that if policymakers wanted to learn something from elsewhere they would choose to look at what the governments of Mauritius or Singapore are doing, not Cuba. As far as healthcare and economic prosperity are concerned there is a great deal to learn from the policies being followed in Singapore. And when it comes to relationships between government, business and the population in general, Mauritius seems to have found a way to utilise the talents of all its people to the best advantage of everyone. Their decisions were based on reality.

In my own business life I made a bad decision in 1997 when I sold a majority share in Black Like Me to a multinational company. My motivation was for our company to benefit from their well-established distribution network and marketing resources. Unfortunately we did not achieve the synergies I expected and the business was sliding backwards. Alien systems and controls were being instituted that added to costs but not to sales. Having done a reality check, I decided to negotiate a termination of the 'marriage', and ended up buying back the business two years later. Reality, not wishful thinking, had to be my guide.

Can our politicians not similarly see where they have made mistakes, do a reality check, and change direction? Do they not realise, for instance, that the talents of all the country's people must be fully utilised to make South Africa a prosperous and peaceful country?

If you look around the world for good leadership of a country you will have difficulty in finding a better example than the late Lee Kuan Yew of Singapore. Lee Kuan Yew became Prime Minister of a poor underdeveloped island of Singapore and turned it into the economic powerhouse it is today. Singapore has an excellent private/public healthcare system and the life expectancy of Singaporeans at birth is 82 years compared to the 53 years of South Africans. Singapore has a GDP per capita of $60,000 compared to South Africa's $11,000, and an unemployment rate of 2% compared to our 36.1%. So what kind of leadership gives you such results?

Would Lee Kuan Yew have introduced a national minimum wage at a time of massive unemployment? Never! Would he have told struggling employers to pay more than the wage they were already paying, which would make them employ less workers? No, he based his policies on reality! Does the government really believe the International Labour Organisation (ILO) representatives who are telling us that establishing a national minimum wage will be good for the economy? Or do they actually know that the ILO is talking rubbish and that if the price of labour increases the buyers will buy less of it and not more and our mass unemployment will increase.

There is no way you can force employers to pay salaries that they cannot afford. So what happens? They will not employ. And when you do employ someone and they do not deliver, you struggle to get rid of them. Why then take that risk. Business on its own is already a risk. We simply need to create a high employment market so that employers know that when they do not pay someone enough they are going to move next door. This is not rocket science, in that employers know they cannot hire and fire randomly after investing in people, because this costs money and time. No employer anywhere in the world would want to employ people just to exploit them. From a logical point of view it does not make sense. Because once you employ someone, for that person to be valuable to you they must be trained, and you do not want to lose people and continually train new people. For you to really stabilise your business, you need loyalty. That is where I believe we make a terrible mistake by ignoring the basic fundamentals of how an economy works. An economy works on the basis of creating entrepreneurs who must be able to employ people where it makes commercial sense. If it does not, then people do not employ.

When I visit less privileged communities I notice the levels of unemployment and the desperation of people, which many of us do. It is actually quite scary. It hurts me that I am unable to assist them. The only way I can assist them is to engage the law makers to understand the devastating effects of our current legislative framework. The responsibility lies with Parliament. They are the ones that developed and approved this legislative framework. They need to understand and appreciate the fact that South Africa is not made out of two million union members. It is made out of fifty million people and all of them are stakeholders. I think that when we come out with legislation, we should make sure we come up with something that is equitable to the fifty million South Africans and not the minority.

As it is, we have 8.7 million unemployed people (36.1% of the potential workforce) in this country. Is the government seriously going to implement a policy that increases that number? Does a reality check not tell them that if you implement the same minimum wage in urban and rural areas, where there is already a low demand for labour, people will definitely lose their jobs? Do they want to cause an 'Arab Spring'? Is that the only kind of reality check that will cause them to change direction? Why consult the ILO? Why not find out from our small and poor employers how many people they will have to fire to stop from going bankrupt themselves? Short-term interventions to create income, like grants, may be necessary. However, it destroys the dignity of our people if we see it as a long-term solution. It can never be a sustainable way of addressing our social issues. Dignity and determining one's own future are principles I believe in passionately.

South Africa's political leaders need to start basing their decisions on reality, and stop basing them on wishful thinking. The survival of the country depends on it!

Herman Mashaba is the Executive Chairperson of Lephatsi Investments; the Founder and CEO of Leswikeng Minerals and Energy; Founder of the beauty products company Black Like Me; and former Chair of the Free Market Foundation. His autobiography entitled *Black Like You* was published in 2013. In his book he shares his growing-up years in Ga-Ramotse, close to Hammanskraal, and how he started selling hair products out of the boot of his car. Herman was elected executive mayor of Johannesburg in August 2016.

Head In The Clouds and Feet On The Ground

Pfungwa Serima

Article published in Sake Beeld on 15 October 2016.
Translated from Afrikaans. Used with permission

Barely two years ago, foreign businesses and analysts were hailing Africa as the world's economic miracle. With economic, political and social reforms sweeping the continent, a burgeoning middle class and growth rates hovering around the 6% mark, people were queuing up for a slice of a $1 trillion opportunity. Today, that picture might appear less appealing to some. Epidemic challenges have swept various countries, especially in West Africa. Across the continent, instability and conflict are either simmering just below the surface. Or worse, bursting out into the open. Between strikes, extremist activities, economic turmoil and political unrest, the African dream might be looking a bit threadbare right now.

Nobody said it would be easy. But for the businesses that are prepared to face the storm and manage the volatility afflicting the continent, there are still huge rewards to be had from doing business in Africa. You just have to be alive to the opportunities and avoid the pitfalls.

As the head of a multinational company that is deeply committed to Africa and its people, I believe firmly that this phase will pass. What is needed at times like this is the ability to manage volatility – something that companies in commodity markets are already familiar with. You do this by having an ear to the ground; have solid relationships with your partners and customers; and as much real-time information as you can get your hands on to make informed predictions and decisions.

The most important component to understanding the continent and its ways is time. When foreign businesses go into a country or a region with preconceived templates and notions, chances are they will miss the opportunity to truly understand how to work and collaborate with governments, potential partners, and potential customers.

Here is the best-kept non-secret to always consider. Africa is a large continent. One size does not fit all. Business is done very differently in Ethiopia than in Nigeria. You will never know Africa based on a PowerPoint presentation. You must immerse yourself into the continent and experience business on the ground, face to face. Choose a few key destinations. Spend time there. Not just for business, but to learn and experience. Engage people in business and on the street. This is the only way to understand the rhythm of the region and understand how business is conducted on the continent.

Of course there are challenges. In many regions, the lack of infrastructure and political instability means that cash is king. This will have a fundamental effect on the way you are paid, or intend to pay, for products and services. You need to stay hands-on. C-suites need to own relationships on the ground. If you're going to try and manage the business by remote control because you think a region is unstable, you are looking at a sure-fire recipe for failure.

I am often asked about the best country on the continent regarding opportunities and stability. There are many options. South Africa will always be right up there, and remains a key launch pad into the continent for many businesses. Angola's a great gateway not only into Lusophone Africa, but into Portugal as well. Nigeria, in spite of its challenges, is the largest economy on the continent and has immense strategic importance to West Africa and the continent as a whole. Ghana is stable, and a relatively easy place to conduct business. While Kenya is experiencing some political unrest, it remains a well-structured country with a strong political agenda. Morocco is emerging strongly as a gateway to West Africa for many European businesses and has created some promising partnerships with English- and French-speaking West African companies. Again, each area has its own regional rhythm of business engagement.

Leadership through volatility requires you to think beyond borders. From an African perspective, we need to drive growth across the continent. We need to start producing home-grown goods and services that our own people will use. We need to think about how we accelerate industries that impact larger geographic areas, thus uplifting more people, communities and smaller businesses that can capitalise on the downstream economic growth. It is Africa doing business with Africa, supported by the many foreign investors who want to contribute to our prosperity.

For us this means delivering a succinct value proposition. And for Africa right now, the Cloud is adding considerably to this task. The Cloud does not require any huge upfront investment. It allows us to be flexible and scalable in what we offer our customers, and what they in turn offer to their customers. It opens doors to locally-relevant, locally-built and locally-developed innovation. Most of all, the Cloud is a great platform to deliver fast, accurate business information and analysis that helps businesses chart their way through unpredictable waters. The Cloud can truly enable Africa to become a connected, networked economy one day.

Feet on the ground, heads in the Cloud. That's the way to do business in Africa right now.

Pfungwa Serima is the Executive Chair of SAP Africa. He is responsible for SAP's strategic direction on the continent. Previously he was the Executive Head of SAP Africa. He holds a degree in business studies and computer science.

SECTION 6
THE FUTURE OF LEADERSHIP

Chapter 9

LOOKING AHEAD

The Future of Leadership

Andrew J Johnson and Theo H Veldsman

In closing our brief excursion into *Building Leadership Talent* it is worthwhile repeating some key assertions we made in the opening chapter:

- leadership is under severe scrutiny, and;
- leadership is in the overheating crucible of a reframed/reframing world that is in the throes of fundamental and radical transformation, hence; and
- the search is on for better and different leadership, in the present and going into the future.

Going into the future, the need for organisations to have an ongoing, deliberate, comprehensive and in-depth conversation about leadership is an imperative if they want not merely to survive but also to thrive sustainably.

In this chapter we would like to gaze into the crystal ball by posing the question: If there is a need for better and different leadership going into the future, what would it look like with the conditions attached to such future-fit leadership?

To this end we explore the features of the growing crisis around leadership; the unfolding, future contextual leadership challenges; profiling the "context fit" leadership of the future; effective leadership engagement with the future context through Skilful Improvisation; and finally, the implications of Skilful Improvisation for growing and developing future-fit leadership.

Features of the Growing Leadership Crisis

Some of the important features of the growing leadership crisis that will have a significant impact on future leadership are:

- *Leadership no longer has any place to hide*. Leaders are in the public eye and under public scrutiny constantly because of the power of social media, and more stringent and expanding corporate governance requirements and demands.
- *Accelerating mistrust, anger towards, suspicion of, disillusionment in, and sense of alienation from, institutional leadership*, whether in business, the public sector, or in politics. There is a growing general public perception that "they are in it for themselves and their own enrichment. People and institutions are merely the means to satisfy their ego-centric needs, wants and purposes."
- *Greater and unrealistic expectations for "leadership on steroids"*. There is little patience with new leaders taking time to settle into and acclimatise to their new roles. The pressure is for instant delivery from the word "go", often against unreasonable deliverables, goals and standards. In many instances, the leadership role expectations from stakeholders are unclear and ambiguous, resulting in decreasing leadership tenures, and higher frequencies of derailment and burnout.
- The *emergence of more spontaneous leadership* in more places, at more times and by more people, the growing trend of "leaderless revolutions". These revolutions are fuelled

by the multiplication and mobilisation power of social media in the hands of everyone, everywhere, anytime. The spontaneous revolutions are blossoming around issues regarding globalisation, climatic warming, technological innovation, religious "holy wars", and demographic displacements like the European refugee crisis. Recent examples of such "leaderless" movements include the #arabspring movements of the Middle East; the #occupy movements in North America and Europe; and #mustfall movements in the South African higher education sector.

- The ***growing cancer of toxic leaders, followers and organisations*** because of the fanatical worshipping of unfettered individualism and egocentricity to the detriment of the pursuit common good; the rampant growth in personal self-interest and self-love (in other words, narcissism); putting "Me Pty Ltd" at the centre; the weakening of the overarching authority of commonly accepted ethical values and norms, also because of value clashes resulting from increasing multicultural settings; and weak followers unable and unwilling to challenge toxic leadership courageously and fiercely.

Unfolding Future Leadership Contextual Challenges

Against the backdrop of the above features of the growing leadership crisis, what are the most apparent unfolding future contextual leadership challenges? We would like to explore these challenges in terms of the conceptual framework given in Figure 9.1, constructed around the relationships in which a leader is embedded.

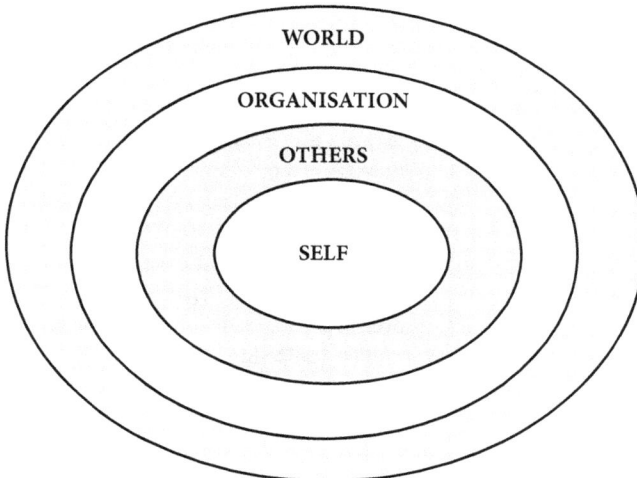

Figure 9.1 Leadership in relationship with the World, Organisation, Others and Self

According to the framework given in Figure 9.1, the leader's success resides in successfully connecting, nurturing and maintaining four interdependent, critical relationships – each with their unique interacting leadership challenges, demands and requirements – with the World; one's Organisation; Others; and Self. Each of the four relationship of leadership will be discussed in turn from a futuristic perspective. Though discussed separately and sequentially, the four relationships form an organic, systemic whole; are in constant reciprocal interaction; and form dynamic patterns, whether vicious or virtuous.

World

Much has been written and spoken about the VUCA World context of Volatility, Uncertainty, Complexity and Ambiguity, expanded here by ourselves to VICCAS: a World of increasing Variety, Interdependence (that is, connectivity), Complexity, Change, Ambiguity, Seamlessness and Sustainability. The counter, "dark" side of the above VICCAS features must also be considered: Over-standardisation, Over-dependency, Over-simplification, Over-formalisation, Over-control, Over-specialisation and Over-concentration. Going forward, the expectation is that the VICCAS Context will intensify.

The key challenges of the VICCAS Context are:

- Pressures arising from **macro destructive and threatening global, socio-economic dynamics invading the global village**, such as wealth concentration in the hands of a few "Haves"; the significantly growing income gap; the relative impoverishment of the middle class; growing structural unemployment because of the Fourth Industrial Revolution (see below); and population displacement because of climatic change and value clashes (see below). The sensitive, interwoven fabric and tapestry of the World – the playing field of leadership – is being torn apart.

- Social media **fragmenting the world into "e-suburbs" of vast global (radicalised) interest groups** talking only to themselves in self-referential ways in self-created echo chambers; radical group recruitment via the Internet; the global tsunami waves of fads and fashions, uninformed opinions and views engulfing the world; the snowballing generation of vast amounts of unvalidated data, information and knowledge feeding and swaying public opinion; parochial, selective views fed by search engines, for example, Google's search engines defining siloed realities for people. Those who have to be led are "disappearing" and becoming faceless in cyberspace through virtualisation and digitisation.

- **Vast technological innovation**, characterised by an exponential rate of change in and merging of multiple technologies across diverse domains such as the physical, digital, and biological manifested in, for example, Artificial Intelligence (AI), robotics, DNA sequencing, the Internet of Things (iot), driverless vehicles, 3D-printing, nanotechnology, biotechnology, big data, materials science, energy storage, and quantum computing. Digitisation and emails are replacing direct face-to-face leadership. It is believed that machines and systems are taking over, replacing people. Against the backdrop of keeping up with technological innovation, future leadership will have to align effectively in real-time technology, people, and working mode continuously relative to the strategic intent they are pursuing.

- Global fundamental **value system clashes and tensions** creating deep fault lines and schisms in communities, organisations and societies. Future leadership will need to build common, shared value spaces enabling diverse people to collaborate for the benefit and common good of all.

- The increasing **untrammelled power of big global corporates** – some bigger than states – leveraged from their control over vast resources globally, pressurising governments, institutions and stakeholders to "toe their line" in order to suit their parochial, narrow, corporate interests. The resources can be moved at the click of a mouse. The challenge to leadership is to move beyond narrow corporate self-interest and adopt a corporate social investment, common good, and a perspective infusing all of the corporate's thinking, decisions and actions.

- The growing **mismatch of global institutions** such as the United Nations (UN), World Bank, IMF, the International Court of Justice, International Criminal Court, and Interpol to oversee and deal in globally representative ways with the increasing contextual complexity of the World. Increasingly these institutions are becoming too simple for, and too unrepresentative of, the complexifying World. The leadership challenge is the re-creation of the existing, and the setting up of newly conceived, institutions matched to the requisite contextual complexity of the VICCAS Context.

Organisation

Against the features of the VICCAS Context, organisations (including institutions) to be led in the future will be facing at least the following challenges:

- The heightened *vulnerability of the organisation's reputation and brand* to social media used for mobilisation against organisations by lobby/interest/pressure groups. Future leadership will have to be a master of the social media, and dominate this communication in space-time.
- The *disruption of traditional business models* because of virtualisation and digitalisation, for example, Amazon, e-Bay, and the on-demand economy driven by the emergence of applications (apps)-based organisations, for example, Uber and airbnb. Future leadership will have to question their existing business model on a continuous basis from first principles.
- The *deconstruction of big corporates* into smaller, highly autonomous, network-based business units in order to instil corporates with nimbleness, agility, client centricity, and responsiveness. The leadership of the future will have to be a networker and alliance and partner builder. He/she will have to be outstanding at building deep and robust relationships.
- Increasing pressure for *demographic representivity* regarding race, gender and culture at all leadership levels from board-level down the organisation, reflective of the organisation's chosen operating arena. Diversity sensitivity will be essential for future leadership.
- Globalisation, enabled by digitisation and virtualisation, will force organisations and leadership to adopt a *global mindset* manifested in thinking globally but acting locally.
- Organisations and their leadership will need to be *future centric* by visiting the future in order to create previously unimaginable, desirable futures. They will then have to return to the present to realise that future. Merely extrapolating from the present into the future, and applying past success recipes, will be a cause of certain extinction for organisations.
- *Disruptive innovation* because of the Fourth Industrial Revolution will necessitate the ongoing re-invention of organisations in terms of client needs, products/services, markets, and modes of delivery. Organisations will be in a constant state of flux. Future leadership will have to be relentless innovators, entrepreneurs and risk takers.
- The *increasing "algorithmisation" of professional knowledge, expertise and decision-making*, enabling para-professionals and users to take over work previously reserved for and claimed by professionals such as medical doctors, lawyers, chartered accounts, and psychologists.
- The *global demand for talent* appropriate to the VICCAS Context will lead to quicker promotion of leaders, resulting in less "intelligent" and mature leaders (see below) in senior and executive positions.
- The VICCAS Context will impose the imperative to shift from *the all-knowing, all-powerful single leader* to *shared (or distributive) leadership and the creation of leadership communities* in organisations, operating beyond hierarchy and function. This will enable the organisation to address more effectively the "wicked" challenges, problems and issues of the VICCAS Context.

Others

Some of the more important future challenges with respect to others are:

- The *range and diversity of stakeholders* of organisations and leaders will grow by leaps and bounds, also because of some of the above discussed trends and leadership challenges, such as the power of social media. Leadership will have to be knowledgeable about the diverse and conflicting needs of multiple stakeholders, including shareholders, the board, employees, suppliers, customers, regulators, competitors and the communities in which they operate, as well as the dynamics infusing each and among one another.
- In the VICCAS context there will be a *growing sense of disempowerment among stakeholders*, and consequently growing feelings among them of being helpless, threatened, anxious and angry. There will be a fervent, mounting, search for "the leader who can save us", creating the potential for followers to be vulnerable to leader exploitation and toxicity.
- The growing ambiguity with regard to *commonly accepted ethical values and norms*, also because of value clashes arising out of the growth in multicultural settings, giving rise to a greater need for value-based leadership, and to build on the "should" and "right". This leadership will need to focus not only on ethical leadership but also on creating a better society and world for present and future generations. Future leadership will have to be imbued by a moral consciousness, compass and courage leveraged from a transcendental leadership stance, namely "why?" leadership.
- The *growing power of public opinion*, solicited by ongoing surveys and referenda, and resulting in the *rise of opportunistic leadership* playing to the grandstand without a firm point of view, and acting without integrity. The need would be for future leadership acting with integrity from a clearly selected position.
- The employee base of organisations shifting to a *significant number of temporary/part time/contract workers* – many merely linked to the organisation through the Internet or an app – who have no real stake in and long-term commitment to the organisation. The challenge to future leadership would be how to engender high levels of engagement from these employees who in many cases have highly sought-after specialist skills.

Self

The challenges emerging from the above will require the future leader to dig much deeper into him-/herself, even though already being overstretched. Specific to the leader, at least the following major future challenges can be distinguished:

- The *constant onslaught on the leader's identity*: who and what am I?; what do I stand for?; what do I want to achieve?; to what end, and for whose benefit?
- The *rapid unlearning of a fixation on past success recipes*; being seduced by transient fads and fashions, and/or the fervent search for "silver bullets" propagated by snake-oil salespersons.
- More *frequent and widespread leadership transitions* requiring constant transitional adjustments by the leader. Leaders will have to be equipped with strong transition strategies and capabilities.
- A *tuned-in-ness to the vulnerability to succumb to toxic leadership*, arising out of the worshipping of individualism and giving rise to self-love; unclear, ambiguous, and conflicting values; the greying of ethics; and toxic friendly followers.
- Leaders running the risk of falling into the trap of *self-protective, "spin-doctoring" conduct* to protect themselves against relentless, merciless public exposure.

- A significantly greater likelihood and frequency of **burnout and organisational derailment** because of contextual pressures and unclear/unrealistic leadership expectations and demands by stakeholders. Leadership resilience will be a key future capability.

"Context Fit"-Leadership for the Future

A cursory scan of the contextual challenges discussed above, highlights the sizeable and seemingly overwhelming contextual demands on leaders going into the future. Leading in this unfolding new world is somewhat, in the words of Hixonia Nyasulu, Chairman of the women-controlled Ayavuna Women's Investments, "like playing tennis in the dark with unknown opponents, unexpected balls, unclear tennis court lines, and unpredictable weather". Equally, there are the possibly bewildering myriad leadership capabilities seemingly necessary to navigate and lead in the VICCAS Context, as elucidated above.

This situation could potentially leave an existing and/or aspiring leader deeply discouraged, with the natural, spontaneous response to withdraw, succumb or fight, instead of engaging positively. Going into the future, we submit that what is required is not a "silver bullet" set of specific capabilities, all needed at the same time in order to produce the "super" leader, able to be fully in charge at all times and under all circumstances; instead, the need will be rather to appreciate situation-specific leadership requirements and in this way identify, grow and develop context-fit leadership. Additionally, a community of leaders should be established, people who are able to lead effectively in a given/expected context through complementary, shared leadership, supplying collectively all of the necessary capabilities within and across situations.

Furthermore, in going into the future, a long-term, complex, and not short-term, mechanistic, vantage point to leadership should be adopted. Such a vantage point will enable us to re-imagine in a holistic, organic, integrated and dynamic way at a truly deep level a leader as a whole person embedded in his/her fourfold relationships with the World, Organisation, Others and Self, which will have to be dynamically and simultaneously aligned in real time.

Going Wide: Future-fit Leadership Capabilities Domains

Based on the above "design criteria", we would like to submit that contextual future-fit leadership will consist of five interdependent capability domains:

- *Able:* The hard and soft capabilities necessary to perform competently relative to contextual demands. The deployment of the required capabilities needs to be infused with the necessary qualities that will bring about hope, passion, caring, harmony, faith, confidence efficacy, courage and perseverance among followers, the psychosocial capital essential for followers to deal with the VICCAS Context effectively.
- *Intelligent:* Leadership who can observe, think, judge, act, learn and reflect with a growing understanding as they engage – conceptually and practically – with the VICCAS Context through converting experiences into information, information into knowledge, and knowledge into wisdom. The total "intelligence" (or meta-intelligence) of an excellent leader will consist of the five interdependent intelligence modes of Intra- and Interpersonal, Systemic, Ideation, Action, and Contextual Intelligence.
- *Mature:* Leadership able to engage consistently in relevant, productive, meaningful and constructive and uplifting ways with Self, Others, the Organisation, and the World.
- *Ethical:* Leaders and leadership who do the right thing for the right reasons in the right way in the right place and the right time with the right persons, that is, the "Should Do", the "Right thing".

- **Authentic:** Leaders and leadership which nurture and affirm the dignity, worth and efficacy of an individual(s), concurrently creating enabling, empowering, and meaningful work experiences.

Specific Future-fit Leadership Capabilities

Given the need for able, intelligent, mature, ethical and authentic leadership, required by the VICCAS Context, Figure 9.2 provides summarised clusters of suggested, more important capabilities ("Can Dos") for future-fit leadership, as per the leadership relationship dimensions discussed above – World, Organisation, Others, and Self. All of these capabilities are infused by the five capability domains of ability, intelligence, maturity, ethics and authenticity, as outlined above.

LEAD IN WORLD	LEAD ORGANISATION
• Agility • Responsiveness • Learning to learn • Systemic, integral thinking • Cross-cultural sensitivity • Purpose and meaning creation	• Political savvy • Risk taking • Disciplined execution • Collaboration and networking • Professional/technical expertise
Leadership who is able; intelligent; mature; ethical and authentic	
• Authenticy • Integrity • Resilience • Inquisitive and curious • Deep thinking • Humility	• Caring • Diversity sensitivity • Stature • Active listening • Empathy • Personal visibility
LEAD SELF	LEAD OTHERS

Figure 9.2 Clusters of suggested, more important capabilities for future-fit leadership

Effective Leadership Engagement with the Future Context through Skilful Improvisation

It should be clear that even when one distils the future-fit capabilities required by leaders – as per Figure 9.2 – to respond effectively to the VICCAS challenges, the list is daunting and intimidating. Therefore, as suggested earlier, one should rather adopt a situational appreciation for the contextual, relevant application of particular capabilities. Such an approach may then lead one to think of effective leadership as an act of "Skilful Improvisation". Perhaps as the futurist, Alvin Toffler, points out, a "new" type of leader is called for, one who depends less on his/her intellectual and technical skills, and is instead one who is open to learning new things, unlearning old things that no longer serve, and relearning some things of value that have been forgotten. In this case, "effectiveness" can be defined as the extent to which a leader is able to achieve his/her intended consequences in a certain context. If leadership is action, it implies that such action can be effective or ineffective relative to the context concerned. Skilful Improvisation entails enabling and empowering leadership to re-invent him-/herself continuously in real time as contextual leadership challenges, demands and requirements shift, expectedly and unexpectedly.

Conceiving of leadership as Skilful Improvisation accepts certain future-fit capabilities will be required to lead effectively in the unfolding Context. In order to do so, leadership will have to develop – holistically and organically – deep capabilities with regard to all of the relationships he/she is embedded in across the five critical capability domains discussed above: ability, intelligence, maturity, ethics, and authenticity. The development of such deep capabilities will require fundamentally deep self-introspection and reflection because the barriers to true leadership effectiveness, organisational change, and excellence reside fundamentally inside the individual leader.

We contend that the VICCAS Context faced by leadership we have sketched in *Building Leadership Talent* will only become worse. It is quite possible that by the time we have developed our leaders in what we consider the "necessary" capabilities, they will already have become outdated. Skilful Improvisation appears to be best suited to address the chaotic VICCAS Context adequately: the insight and will to be able to "read" the situation as a leader correctly; to exercise the right judgement; to choose from a set of capabilities such as those given in Figure 9.2 those that are situationally relevant skills as demanded by the task, people, organisational and contextual requirements; reflecting-in-action both on his/her own state of mind and the backtalk[1] of the situation, in order to perform effectively.

Impossible? Then perhaps leadership growth and development should be informed by the approach of artists. The above is precisely what jazz artists do so well.[2] Leaders know very well that life more often than not does not turn out in the way one has planned it. What if our thinking and doing are agile enough to bend with what we get served, analogous to the way in which jazz artists think and act. The jazz band may be playing a piece that they have rehearsed well, then unexpectedly someone makes a mistake. Now what if the thinking in that moment is: "There are no mistakes"; certainly not a "mistake" by someone else. Only the "mistake" of an inadequate in-the-moment response to the backtalk of the situation.[3]

Implications of Skilful Improvisation for Growing and Developing Future-fit Leadership

Skilful improvisation requires very deep personal development. Because leaders have little control over their external (chaotic) context, and quite likely become drained by its demands, it stands to reason that leaders will have to find resources internally in themselves. Such growth and development will include capacity growth and development in respect of the capability range indicated earlier (see Figure 9.2) but first and foremost in his/her relationship to him-/herself.

Going deep

This is essential because there is a blindness in all human beings through years of socialisation that necessitates that such growth and development drill deeper into the deepest layers of leaders' lived world if they are to be capacitated for the intensifying VICCAS Context. Figure 9.3 depicts the respective layers making up the leader's lived world, from "deep" to "shallow".

Visible, tangible
Action learning

Layer 6: Everyday Lived
Experiences and Actions

Layer 5: Capabilities

Layer 4: Style and Attitude

Layer 3: Decision Making

Framework

Layer 2: Value

Orientation

Layer 1: Worldview

Invisible, intangible
Double-loop learning, learning to learn

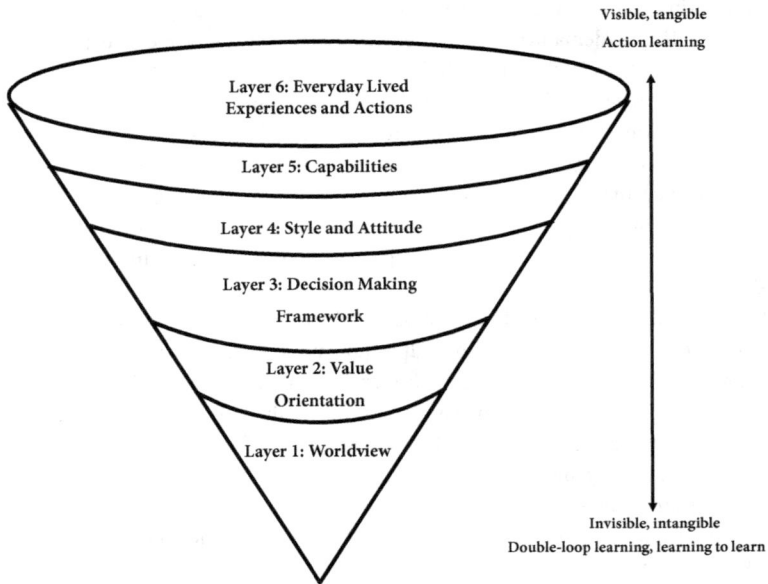

Figure 9.3 Layers making up the leader's lived world

Analogous to the building of a house, future-fit leadership growth and development have to commence with the deep Layer 1: Worldview (or Mental Model), and then proceed progressively to the more shallow layers in a "building onto" manner. Learning in this way will help the leader to bring his socially programmed blindness to conscious reflection, and develop new pathways towards effective leadership, including purposefulness: an authentic balanced disposition to the needs of others (= all stakeholders), the organisation, and the world. Learning approaches and methods will have to be employed by organisations that elicit valid information and knowledge about what individuals think and do at deep layers, because the default pattern of individuals is to employ defensive reasoning. We espouse leadership effectiveness, but as human beings we lack the ability to produce such holistic inside-out development. In addition, we are unaware of this serious, future-compromising limitation.

Bringing about deep learning

How do we effect this deep learning? As indicated earlier, one cannot simply focus on changing Layers 6: Everyday lived experiences and 5: Capabilities (see Figure 9.3). Layers 5 and 6 learning tend to break down when people experience stress because stress triggers default conduct. One has to change the underlying layers, in particular Layers 1 to 3, that drive the conduct, to Layer 6. Skilful improvisation requires drawing on deep, internal personal resources that this type of development endeavours to develop.

The knowledge organisations produce in our leadership growth and development programmes must be in the service of enabling leadership action with regard to Layer 6. Two expressions of such learning are (i) *double-loop learning*, aimed at getting to the mental models comprising underlying beliefs, values and attitudes (Layers 1 to 4) that perpetuate ineffective leadership action, in conjunction with (ii) *action learning*, focusing on conduct change through reflection on real stakeholder and organisational challenges (in other words, Layers 5 and 6) (see Figure 9.3). In the words of Argyris, Putnam, and McLain Smith,[4] methods will have to be employed "to make known what is known so well that we no longer know it, … so that it might be critiqued, … and to make known what is unknown, … the discovery of alternatives so that they too might be critiqued". Skilful improvisation contains such reflexive qualities.

Bridging the science-practice gap

Such leadership growth and development, based on sound scientific principles, will have the potential to respond adequately to bridging the perennial, ongoing science–practice gap. *Building Leadership Talent* abounds with many such exemplars. In practice, this growth and development in organisations can be self-driven, technology-enabled, classroom- based, experiential and/or coaching, provided it conforms to its purposes: deep, inside-out growth and development from Layer 1 "upwards" towards Layer 6. Then and only then will organisations be preparing and delivering the right leadership in the right numbers at the right time and place, able, willing and empowered to perform effectively within the VICCAS Context.

Fundamental to this leadership growth and learning will be the need for academics and development practitioners to do less "esoteric", practice-estranged work that results in the growing gap between theory – the proverbial ivory tower – and practice. Within the VICCAS Context, real action research partnerships between academic institutions and business/non-governmental institutions/public sector are essential, focusing on leadership growth and development that is useful to leadership in the moment of action where it matters and will make a real difference. In other words, leadership growth and development that is characteristic of reflective practice, reflecting-in- and -on-action. Given financial pressures, organisations need to place a much greater emphasis on evidence-based, actionable knowledge to drive their change efforts. The speed of practice-referenced and -informed research delivery by academics will have to match the speed of change in the practical world. Otherwise, academics and academic institutions will rapidly become irrelevant to a VICCAS Context "running away" from them. They will become the extinct dinosaurs going into the future.

Conclusion

Having explored tomorrow's VICCAS Leadership Context with its features resulting in "wicked" leadership challenges, issues and problem, answering the remaining ultimate question posed in the Introduction is: "Is there a future for leadership?" Yes, there is a future for leadership, but it is conditional on:

- A *deep understanding of the unfolding VICCAS Context* going into the future in terms of leadership's fourfold relationships with the World, Organisation, Others and Self;
- *Adoption of a complexity vantage point* to leadership;
- From this complexity perspective, *re-imagine at a deep level leaders in a holistic, organic, integrated and dynamic way as a whole person,* in terms of their ability, intelligence, maturity, ethics and authenticity, as embedded in their fourfold relationships, all of which have to be dynamically aligned simultaneously in real time;
- Enabling and empowering leaders to engage with the Context through *Skilful Improvisation*;
- *Growing and developing leadership from the inside-out*, commencing with the deeper layers of leadership's lived world: Layer 1: Worldview through double-loop learning, progressing through action learning towards Layer 6: Everyday Lived Experiences and Actions; and
- *Forming vibrant two-way interactions between the academic and practice worlds,* producing just-in-time, evidence-based, actionable knowledge to drive change efforts to make leaders future-fit.

What a challenge lies ahead of all of us to make it happen in a world that is in desperate need of Building Leadership Talent in order to ensure a sustainable, flourishing future for all.

Endnotes

1   "The situation talks back, the [leader] listens, and as he appreciates what he hears, he reframes the situation once again": *cf.* Schön, DA. 1983. *The reflective practitioner.* New York, NY: Basic Books.

2   *cf.* Also (a) Warren Bennis on jazz and leadership: "I used to think that running an organization was equivalent to conducting a symphony orchestra. But I don't think that's quite it; it's more like jazz. There is more improvisation"; (b) the leadership development training, styled on UK Channel 4s "Whose line is it anyway?", *Workplace IMPROV*, designed by stand-up comedian, Nadiem Solomon. The fundamental rule in this training is "pay attention".

3   Harris, S. 2011. *There are no mistakes on the bandstand.* TEDSalon NY2011.

4   Argyris, C, Putnam, R & McLain Smith, D. 1985. *Action science: concepts, methods, and skills for research and intervention.* San Francisco, CA: Jossey-Bass Inc. 237.

INDEX

www.ingramcontent.com/pod-product-compliance
Lightning Source LLC
Chambersburg PA
CBHW061330220326
41599CB00026B/5112